BARCELONA
POCKET GUIDE

TOP 10 ATTRACTIONS

LA RAMBLA
A lively and entertaining place by day or night. See page 25.

SAGRADA FAMÍLIA
Gaudí's unfinished masterpiece. See page 55.

FUNDACIÓ JOAN MIRÓ
This museum showcases an exceptional body of the artist's work. See page 69.

MONESTIR DE PEDRALBES
A peaceful haven. See page 73.

MUSEU PICASSO

The largest collection of the artist's work outside Paris. See page 45.

CASA BATLLÓ

One of the city's famous *modernista* buildings. See page 50.

PALAU DE LA MÚSICA CATALANA

Fabulous mosaics, tiles and sculpture. See page 46.

PALAU NACIONAL

This monumental building houses 1,000 years of Catalan art. See page 67.

BARRI GÒTIC

The sombre Gothic Cathedral is at the heart of this old quarter. See page 32.

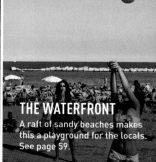

THE WATERFRONT

A raft of sandy beaches makes this a playground for the locals. See page 59.

A PERFECT DAY

9.00am

La Rambla

Get an early start on La Rambla to enjoy it under the morning Mediterranean light before the crowds arrive. Pick up your newspaper from a newsstand then pop into La Boqueria market – at its most colourful in the morning – for a proper Catalan breakfast like baby squid and poached eggs at El Quim (see page 106)

12 noon

Santa Maria del Mar church

Over Via Laietana is the Born district. Glimpse the breathtaking interior of Santa Maria del Mar, or sip *una copa de cava* on the terrace of La Vinya del Senyor (see page 108) and admire the church facade.

10.30am

1.30pm

Lunch time

Get into the local rhythm and have a *menú del dia*, three courses at remarkably low rates, in a neighbourhood bar like Rodrigo (see page 106) in Argenteria, or around the Passeig del Born. Another option is to walk 10 minutes to Barceloneta for a paella by the sea at Can Majó (see page 110).

Gothic Quarter

Across La Rambla is the Gothic Quarter. Meander through its shady narrow lanes and palm-filled courtyards. Get the background on today's Old Town at the City History Museum (MUHBA) or break for coffee in the diminutive Meson del Café on Llibreteria.

5.30pm

10.30pm

Explore the Eixample

A session of retail therapy in the modernista setting of the Eixample is recommended for all the family. Those who don't wish to shop can visit a Gaudí building, like La Pedrera or Casa Batlló, or just wander around the area to admire a wealth of decorative details, from stained glass to ceramics, by his contemporaries.

On the town

Round off the day in style just up the road at designer club Ommsession (Rosselló 265), part of award-winning Hotel Omm, where you can rub shoulders with the sleek and beautiful. Alternatively, catch a cab to Mirablau, halfway up Tibidabo hill, and dance till dawn overlooking the city.

3.30pm

8.30pm

Siesta

A gentle stroll along the Passeig Marítim towards the Vila Olímpica, pausing for coffee in one of the waterfront *xiringuitos* (beach bars), is ideal for working off lunch. Then indulge in a taxi back to base for a reviving *siesta*, essential to keep up the pace until the small hours.

Drinks and tapas

Relax at one of the many terrace bars in elegant Rambla Catalunya, or try the eponymous cocktail at Dry Martini (Aribau 162), before going for tapas, the perfect dinner, especially when created by top chef Carles Abellan at Tapas 24 (see page 110).

CONTENTS

◉ Walking Eye App

Your Insight Pocket Guide purchase includes a free download of the destination's corresponding eBook. It is available now from the free Walking Eye container app in the App Store and Google Play. Simply download the Walking Eye container app to access the eBook dedicated to your purchased book. The app also features free information on local events taking place and activities you can enjoy during your stay, with the option to book them. In addition, premium content for a wide range of other destinations is available to purchase in-app.

HOW TO DOWNLOAD THE WALKING EYE APP

Available on purchase of this guide only.
1. Visit our website: www.insightguides.com/walkingeye
2. Download the Walking Eye container app to your smartphone (this will give you access to your free eBook and the ability to purchase other products)
3. Select the scanning module in the Walking Eye container app
4. Scan the QR Code on this page – you will be asked to enter a verification word from the book as proof of purchase
5. Download your free eBook* for travel information on the go

* Other destination apps and eBooks are available for purchase separately or are free with the purchase of the Insight Guide book

INTRODUCTION

Barcelona may be the second city of Spain, locked in eternal rivalry with Madrid, but it ruled an empire long before Spain was even born. Some 2,000 years ago, the Romans, on their way to conquering the whole of Iberia, built a forbidding wall around their settlement on the Mediterranean coast and called it Barcino.

Although a visitor could spend days wandering the Gothic Quarter, an atmospheric tangle of medieval buildings and alleyways where the city's glorious past is palpable, Barcelona is anything but a musty old history lesson. It is a dynamic, densely populated and daringly modern metropolis. Since hosting the 1992 Olympic Games, the city, capital of the autonomous region of Catalonia, has become one of Europe's hottest cities.

Once grimy and grey, with a smelly industrial port that pushed this former maritime power away from the sea, Barcelona has reinvented itself. Badly needed new circulation routes were built, rundown neighbourhoods have been reborn and numerous 'urban spaces', filled with sculpture and greenery, have been created. The airport, railway and metro have been brought up to date, and new hotels, museums and concert halls have sprung up. The most important physical change, though, has been Barcelona's reorientation towards the sea. With a dynamic port that is now one of the busiest cruise-ship stops in Europe, the Olímpic port, a further leisure port at Diagonal Mar, its clean beaches and renowned seafront neighbourhoods, the Catalan capital has succeeded in marrying the seductive pleasures of the Mediterranean with the sophisticated, creative energy of modern Europe. The focus is now on the two main arteries running east-west to the sea, Avinguda Diagonal and Avinguda Paral.lel. The aim is to create a cohesive connection between these two roads and the flourishing port with

Celebrating Catalonia National Day in September

its cruise-ship terminal, and the Forum's trade fair, exhibition and conference venues. Despite recession and the euro crisis the development continues.

CATALAN CULTURE

Barcelona's physical transformation has accompanied a rebirth of Catalan culture, long marginalised – often overtly repressed – by Spanish rulers. The most ruthless aggression came during the Franco dictatorship, which lasted from the Spanish Civil War of 1936–39 until the dictator's death in 1975. Under the 1979 Statute of Autonomy, Catalonia regained a substantial measure of self-government; this was moderately amplified by a new statute approved in 2006. Catalan arts, literature and language are vigorously promoted by the Catalan government. The election of Catalan nationalist Xavier Trias as mayor in 2011 has further boosted the cause.

Reawakened, too, is the pride the Barceloneses take in their city. They are proud of their architecture and design. The man behind much of it is the city's most famous son, Antoni Gaudí (1852–1926), one of the creators of *modernisme*, Catalan Art Nouveau. Gaudí's buildings still startle: his soaring, unfinished cathedral, La Sagrada Família, is his best-known work, but there are scores more in Barcelona. And that's just Gaudí; around the turn of the 20th century, a group of *modernistas*, including Lluís Domènech i Montaner and Josep Puig i Cadafalch, dreamed up the most fanciful buildings their rich imaginations and equally rich patrons would allow. More recent architectural stars include Oriol Bohigas, Enric Ruiz-Geli, Miralles and Tagliabue and a host of international architects like Jean Nouvel, Norman Foster, Richard Rogers, Frank Gehry, Herzog and de Meuron, who have all created new landmarks in the city or have work in progress.

DESIGN AND PRAGMATISM

Barcelona also nurtured the careers of some of the 20th-century's greatest artists – the Catalans Joan Miró and Salvador

SARDANES

The city – and the region – takes its culture seriously. Rituals like the sardana, a traditional dance performed on Saturday evening and Sunday morning in front of the cathedral, and in Plaça Sant Jaume on some Sunday evenings, are held almost sacred. Men, women and children hold hands and form a circle to perform the apparently simple but highly regimented steps. The band, called a cobla, comprising strings, brass and a drum, plays lilting, melancholic tunes as more and more circles form until the entire area is filled with dancers.

Dalí, and also Pablo Picasso, who spent his formative years in the Catalan capital before seeking fame in Paris (Barcelona's Picasso museum has the largest collection of his work outside Paris). Few other cities are as design-mad as Barcelona. The opening of every high-tech museum, bridge and bar is a public event discussed and debated by local people. Couples rush to place their wedding lists at the trendiest design shops, and avant-garde public spaces are analysed thoughtfully and, more often than not, publicly funded.

However, Barceloneses tend to be surprisingly conservative and pragmatic. Spain's industrial juggernaut, Barcelona is serious about work and money. Containing 15 percent of Spain's population (1.6 million in the city itself), Catalonia produces more than 20 percent of the country's GDP and a third of all exports. Catalans have a reputation for being tight with money – a criticism that's a backhanded compliment acknowledging that they know how to earn and manage it.

CATALAN INDEPENDENCE

Barcelona has long been considered different from the rest of Spain, and though visitors can attend a bullfight or flamenco show, this really isn't the place for such typically Spanish practices. The city is famous for its stubborn sense of independence and identity. Catalans have held onto their language tenaciously, defending it against repeated attempts from Castile, and the Franco government, to extinguish it. Above all, they believe Catalonia is a nation, not a mere region. While there are many who would prefer Barcelona

Take a tour

To quickly get the full measure of this dynamic Mediterranean city hop on (and off wherever you want) the Bus Turístic, or go for a walking, bike, boat, scooter or helicopter tour. Check www.barcelonaturisme. com for the latest offers.

to be the capital of an independent, Catalan-speaking nation, the majority of these hard-working people are simply frustrated that so much locally generated wealth is re-routed to Madrid.

All political considerations are cast aside, though, when seemingly the whole of Barcelona takes to the streets just before lunch or in the early evening. La Rambla, a tree-lined boulevard Victor Hugo called 'the most beautiful in the world', is packed with local people and visitors. Boisterous patrons spill out of corner bars, where they've dipped in to eat tapas (an array of snacks that might include a wedge of omelette, sardines, octopus, olives, cheese, chorizo sausage and much more) and have a glass of wine, beer or local cava (sparkling wine that comes from just outside Barcelona). Mime artists strike poses for photos and spare change, and older people take a seat to watch the whole parade stream by.

The Carrer del Lledó, where Barcelona's aristocrats used to live

EXPLORING ON FOOT

Take your cue from local people and La Rambla: Barcelona is an ideal city for walking. Hemmed in by the sea, the River Besòs and hills on two sides, the city is surprisingly manageable. It spills down a gentle slope to the waterfront. Near the water are the Barri Gòtic (Gothic Quarter) and the rest

Bar Marsella, a bohemian absinthe bar in El Raval

of the old city, a labyrinth of streets inhabited for a thousand years. Ancient stones of the Roman city are visible in columns and walls, and you can visit the settlement's original foundations beneath the Museu d'Història de la Ciutat. Barcelona grew out of its original walls, and its modern sectors extend in all directions. The avenues are broad and leafy, punctuated by squares crowded with cafés. The Eixample district, a grid of streets laid out in the 19th century, includes landmark modernista apartment buildings, fashionable boutiques, galleries, restaurants and hotels.

Barcelona is every bit as spirited at night as it is during the day. Residents begin their evenings with tapas and rounds of drinks after work, activities that put dinner off until a fashionably late hour. Ten o'clock is normal but it's not uncommon for Barceloneses to sit down to dinner at midnight. Live-music venues and clubs don't really get going until 2am. Any day of the week, La Rambla pulsates with life into the early hours of the morning. If late-night Barcelona is too wild for your tastes, an evening stroll is also a highlight: the cathedral and other churches, palaces and monuments are all illuminated. The Barri Gòtic retreats into silence, broken only by the animated hollering of late-night revellers or the rumble of skateboards.

A BRIEF HISTORY

Barcelona was originally called Barcino, named after the Carthaginian general and father of Hannibal, Hamilcar Barca, who established a base on the northeastern coast of Iberia in the 3rd century BC. Phoenicians and Greeks had previously settled the area, and Barcino occupied the site of an earlier Celtiberian settlement called Laie. But the Romans, who conquered all of Iberia, left the most indelible marks on Barcelona. They defeated the Carthaginians at Ilipa in 206 BC and ruled Spain for the next 600 years, a period in which Roman law, language and culture took firm root across the peninsula. The Roman citadel in Barcelona, surrounded by a massive wall, occupied high ground where the cathedral, Catalan government building and city hall now stand. From the 1st century AD Christian communities spread throughout Catalonia.

VISIGOTHIC CAPITAL

After the sack of Rome, Visigoths swept into Spain in AD 476. They made Barcelona their capital from 531 until 554, when they moved their power base to Toledo. The invasion of the Moors in 713 brought the Visigothic kingdom to an end, and Catalonia was briefly overrun by the invaders from North Africa. After their defeat beyond the Pyrenees by the Franks in 801, the Moors withdrew to the south, and retained no lasting foothold in Catalonia. Charlemagne's knights installed themselves in the border counties to guard the southern flank of his empire.

A feudal lord, Guifré el Pelós (Wilfred the Hairy) became the Count of

Catalan character

While much of Spain was under Moorish domination, Catalonia remained linked to Europe. This has done much to determine the distinctive Catalan character.

Columbus' riches

In 1493, after Columbus' voyage to the Americas, he was received by the monarchs Ferdinand and Isabella in Barcelona's Royal Palace. Despite the gesture, Castile, the power centre of Spain, exclusively exploited New World riches, to the exclusion of Barcelona.

Barcelona. In 878 he founded a dynasty that would rule for nearly five centuries. He also gave the budding nation its flag of four horizontal red stripes on a gold field, the oldest still in use in Europe. When King Louis V refused to come to their aid against Moorish raiders, the counts of Barcelona declared their independence in 988, a date celebrated as Catalonia's birth as a nation-state. The Catalan nation was soon enlarged through marriage and military adventure, in particular by Ramon Berenguer III, who ruled from 1082 to 1131.

MERCANTILE NATION

Successive generations turned their attention towards the conquest of the Mediterranean basin. Jaume I (1213–76) consolidated control over the Balearic Islands and claimed Valencia. Sicily was annexed in 1282, and over the ensuing century Barcelona reached the peak of its glory. Its mercantilist trade grew rapidly and its territories included Sardinia, Corsica, Naples and Roussillon in southern France.

The Middle Ages, from the late 13th to the 15th century, were a time of great building in Barcelona, giving rise to the cathedral and other great Gothic palaces and monuments. Barcelona served as a channel for the exchange of scientific knowledge and scholarship. The arts flourished, patronised by a vigorous class of artisans, bankers and merchants, including an important Jewish community.

Nascent political institutions appeared, and in 1359 the

Corts Catalanes, or Catalan parliament, which had been meeting irregularly since the 1280s, was officially appointed. A body which later became the Generalitat (government) was set up to regulate financial and political concerns.

SPAIN UNITED

The marriage of Ferdinand of Aragón-Catalonia (Ferrán II to the Catalans) to Isabella of Castile in 1469 joined the two crowns and formed the nucleus of a united Spanish state.

Under the Catholic Monarchs Catalonia was incorporated into Castile. The Catholic church's hard-line Inquisition expelled Jews from Spain and the thriving communities in Barcelona and Girona were particularly badly affected.

King Ferdinand and Queen Isabella greet Columbus in the National Gallery

During the 16th century, a Golden Age for Spain, the political influence of Catalonia and Barcelona declined even further. The Habsburg grandson of Ferdinand and Isabella was anointed Carlos I of Spain in 1516. He inherited the title of Holy Roman Emperor and became Charles V, with Europe-wide duties that gave him little time for Spain. His son, Felipe II, moved the capital of the Spanish empire from Toledo to Madrid.

The maritime empire's glory is showcased in the Museu Marítim

WAR AND RESISTANCE

In 1640, with Spain and France involved in the Thirty Years' War, Catalonia declared itself an independent republic, allied to France. Spanish troops besieged and captured Barcelona in 1651 and after the French defeat in 1659 Catalan territories north of the Pyrenees were ceded to France, fixing the border where it is today. The ensuing years were rife with wars and disputes over succession to the crown, in which Barcelona automatically sided with whoever opposed Madrid.

The worst of these episodes came in the War of the Spanish Succession (1701–14) between the backers of Philip of Anjou, grandson of Louis XIV of France, and the Habsburg claimant, Archduke Charles of Austria. Charles was enthusiastically received when he landed in Catalonia, but Philip, supported by France, won the war and became the first Bourbon ruler, Philip V. After a 13-month siege, on 11 September 1714 the royal army captured and sacked Barcelona. The Catalan

Generalitat was dissolved and the city's privileges abolished. The Ciutadella fortress was built to keep the populace subdued, and official use of the Catalan language was outlawed. Catalonia celebrates this date as its national holiday, the Diada, a symbol of the spirit of nationalist resistance.

Discord within the Spanish government or conflict with foreign powers frequently served as an excuse for Catalan separatists to rise up, though their rebellions were usually summarily squashed. From 1808 to 1814, Spain again became a battleground, with British forces opposing Napoleon in the Peninsular War. Napoleon attacked and destroyed Catalonia's sacred shrine, the monastery at Montserrat.

The spirit of European liberalism was late in reaching Spain. After many reverses, a republic, a constitutional monarchy and a democratic constitution were instituted in 1873. Shortly afterwards, Barcelona was at long last given the right to trade with the colonies of the New World.

INDUSTRIALISATION

Meanwhile, the city had gone about its business, devoting its energies to industrialisation. Barcelona's medieval walls were torn down to make way for an expansion in the mid-19th century. The Eixample district was laid out on a grid of broad avenues where the new industrialists built mansions. Wealthy patrons supported such architects as Antoni Gaudí and Lluís Domènech i Montaner. Prosperity was accompanied by a revival in arts and letters, a period known in Catalan as the Renaixença (Renaissance). The city bid for worldwide recognition with the Universal Exposition of 1888, on the site of the Ciutadella fortress, today's Parc de la Ciutadella.

With the industrial expansion, an urban working class evolved. Agitation for social justice and regionalist ferment created a combustible atmosphere, and the city became the scene of strikes and anarchist violence. The modern Socialist Party and the UGT, Spain's largest trade union, were founded, and industrialists sought Catalan autonomy as a way to be freed from interference from Madrid. In 1914 a provincial government, the Mancomunitat, was formed, uniting the four Catalan provinces – Barcelona, Tarragona, Lleida and Girona. It was dissolved in 1923 by General Primo de Rivera, who established a military dictatorship and banned the Catalan language.

CIVIL WAR

In 1931, the Second Republic was established, and King Alfonso XIII escaped to exile. Catalonia won a charter establishing home rule, restoration of the regional parliament and flag, and recognition of Catalan as the official language. Elements in the Spanish army rebelled in 1936, initiating the brutal Civil War. Many churches in Barcelona were put to the torch by anti-clerical mobs. The firmly Republican city was a rallying point for the International Brigade. Barcelona was one of the last cities to fall to the rebel troops of General Francisco Franco at the war's end in 1939.

The Civil War ended with some 700,000 combatants dead; another 30,000 were executed, including many priests and nuns; perhaps as many as 15,000 civilians were killed in air raids and numerous refugees left the country. Catalonia paid a heavy price in defeat. Franco abolished all regional institutions and established central controls. The Catalan language was proscribed, even

Montjuic Exhibition

Despite the Primo de Rivera dictatorship (1923–30), Barcelona plunged into preparations for another International Exhibition, with monumental buildings and sports facilities on Montjuic hill, many of which can still be seen today. It opened just before the stock market crash of 1929.

in schools and churches. For years, Barcelona received little financial support from Madrid, and Spain remained essentially cut off from the rest of Europe.

1960 ONWARDS

Despite this cultural and political repression and the depressed post-war years, by the 1960s the industrious Catalans were again forging ahead, making this corner of Spain the most successful economically. The traditional textile sector was overtaken by the more prosperous iron, steel and chemical indus-

The Arc de Triomf, built for the 1888 Universal Exposition

tries, which called for man-power, so people from the less prosperous rural regions of Spain flocked to Barcelona. Sprawling suburbs with ugly high-rise buildings mushroomed around the city in an uncontrolled fashion. Franco's government promoted tourism in the 1960s, and crowds from the North began to descend on the Costa Brava. Speculators exploited the coastline but the economy boomed.

The dictatorship ended with Franco's death in 1975. Juan Carlos, grandson of Alfonso XIII, became king and Spain made a rapid and successful transition to democracy. In Catalonia cava flowed in the streets on the day Franco died and the Generalitat was restored as the governing body of the autonomous region. The Catalan language was made official and a renaissance of culture and traditions has followed, seen in literature, theatre, television, films, cultural centres, arts festivals and popular fiestas.

In Barcelona the charismatic Socialist mayor Pasqual Maragall shaped today's modern city by using the 1992 Olympics as an excuse to start a radical programme of urban reform to remedy the years of neglect by central government. The momentum of this drive continued after the Olympics and launched Barcelona into the 21st century under mayor Jordi Hereu. Urban, economic and social refurbishment has been implemented in the 22@ project – approved by the city council in 2000 and still ongoing – clearing old industrial areas such as Poble Nou, improving transport links and making way for high-tech industries and classy new business hotels. The election of the first Catalan Nationalist to hold the post of mayor, Xavier Trias, in 2011, saw the end of 32 years of Socialist leadership and has given a boost to the Catalan population. Despite hard economic times, which are slowing the building process, Barcelona enjoys a high-profile status as a top business and conference centre and ranks high amongst European cities for its quality of life.

Crowds march for Catalan independence

HISTORICAL LANDMARKS

237 BC Carthaginian Hamilcar Barca makes his base at Barcino.

206 BC Romans defeat Carthaginians in Battle of Ilipa.

AD 531–54 Barcelona becomes the capital of the Visigoths.

711 Moorish invasion of Spain. They remain there till 1492.

878 Wilfred (Guifré) the Hairy founds dynasty of counts of Barcelona.

1096–1131 Ramón Berenguer III extends Catalan empire.

1213–76 Jaume I consolidates empire, expands Barcelona.

1359 Corts Catalanes (Parliament of Catalonia) established.

1469 Ferdinand and Isabella unite Aragón and Castile.

1494 Administration of Catalonia put under Castilian control.

1516 Carlos I (Charles V, Holy Roman Emperor) takes throne.

1659 Catalan territories north of Pz`yrenees ceded to France.

1701–14 War of Spanish Succession.

1713–14 Siege of Barcelona by Felipe V's forces; Ciutadella fortress built.

1808–14 Peninsular War between England and France.

1888 Barcelona hosts its first Universal Exposition.

1914 Mancomunitat (provincial government) formed in Catalonia.

1923 General Primo de Rivera sets up dictatorship and bans Catalan language.

1931 Republican party comes to power.

1932 Catalonia granted short-lived statute of independence.

1936–9 Civil War ends in Franco's rule and isolation of Spain.

1975 Franco dies; Juan Carlos becomes king.

1979 Statute of Autonomy; Catalan restored as official language.

1986 Spain joins European Community (European Union).

1992 Barcelona hosts the Olympics.

2006 A new statute is passed, giving Catalonia more autonomy.

2009 High-tech business district 22@ forges ahead successfully.

2011 Xavier Trias of the Catalan Nationalist party is elected mayor.

2014 80 percent of voters say "yes" to Catalonia's separation from Spain in a non-binding November referendum.

2015 Barcelona ranks 15th safest city in the world (*The Economist*).

WHERE TO GO

Barcelona can be approached by neighbourhood or by theme. You can set out to see the Gothic Quarter, Montjuïc hill, or the waterfront, or you can create a tour around the works of Gaudí and *modernisme* or the latest cutting-edge architecture. It's very tempting to try to sandwich everything into your stay, but leave time to get sidetracked in a colourful food market or an alley of antiques shops, or to peek in a quiet courtyard. Take a breather, sit at a pavement café while you linger over a drink, read a newspaper, and watch the people go by.

In the Old Town – Barri Gòtic, La Ribera, El Raval, La Rambla – and the Eixample district, the best way to travel is on foot. For sights further afield, including Montjuïc, Barceloneta and the waterfront, Tibidabo, and two of the top Gaudí attractions, La Sagrada Família and Park Güell, it's best to make use of Barcelona's excellent public transport network – clean and efficient metro, suburban trains, modern buses, funiculars, trams and cable cars – as well as plenty of inexpensive taxis (see page 130). A good map is essential, but it's easy to be fooled by how close things look on paper.

LA RAMBLA

To call **La Rambla** ❶ a street is to do it woeful injustice. Perhaps Europe's most famous boulevard – energetic, artistic, democratic and a touch decadent – it is an intoxicating parade of humanity. You will no doubt want to sample it several times during your stay, despite the crowds. It's at its best in the morning or in the early evening, while in the wee hours it's populated by a motley mix of newspaper sellers, street-sweepers and late-night revellers stumbling back to their apartments and hotels. At all times, be streetwise to avoid pickpockets.

Main entrance to Park Güell

The broad, tree-shaded promenade stretches nearly 1.5km (1 mile) down a gentle incline from the city's hub, Plaça de Catalunya (see page 54), to the waterfront. La Rambla takes its name from an Arabic word meaning a sandy, dry river bed; it was a shallow gully until the 14th century, when Barcelona families began to construct homes nearby. As the area became more populated, the stream was soon paved over. To the north of La Rambla (left as you walk down it) is the Gothic Quarter; to the south, or right, is El Raval.

La Rambla cuts through the centre of the Old Town

CANALETES

The five sections of La Rambla change in character, as they do in name (hence it is often called 'Les Rambles'), as you stroll along. The short **Rambla de Canaletes** at the top, named after the **Font de Canaletes**, the fountain that is one of the symbols of the city, is where crowds pour in from the Plaça de Catalunya or emerge from the metro and railway stations beneath. On Sunday and Monday in football season you'll find noisy knots of fans verbally replaying the games of Barça, Barcelona's beloved football club; if an important match has just been won, watch out for the fireworks. Here, too, begin the newsstands where you can buy a selection of foreign newspapers and magazines, as well as books, a reflection of Barcelona's status as Spain's publishing centre. You'll also see the first of the ubiquitous human statues, along with break-dancers, lookalikes of Barça legends performing football feats, or magicians perform-ing tricks.

Dance troupe on Rambla de les Flors

BIRDS AND FLOWERS

Next is **Rambla dels Estudis**, popularly called **Rambla dels Ocells** (Rambla of the Birds) because here the boulevard becomes an outdoor aviary where winged creatures of all descriptions are sold. When the vendors leave at the end of the day, their cage-lined stalls are folded and shut like wardrobes, with the birds rustling about inside.

Birds give way to flowers in the **Rambla de les Flors**, offi-cially the **Rambla de Sant Josep**. People flock here on 23 April, the feast day of Sant Jordi (St George), patron saint of Catalonia, celebrated as Day of the Book because it is also the anniversary of Cervantes' and Shakespeare's deaths in 1616. A woman traditionally gives her man a book, and a man gives a woman a rose – both of which are available in abundance along La Rambla. Keep an eye peeled on the right side of the road for the delectable *modernista* pastry and chocolate shop, **Escribà** (Antiga Casa Figueres), its fanciful swirls on the out-side a match for the delicacies within. An ideal spot for coffee.

Facing the Rambla is the elegant **Palau de la Virreina**, a grand palace completed in 1778 for the young widow of the viceroy of colonial Peru. The palace is partially open for cultural events and major exhibitions, and houses a branch of the city's Department of Culture where you can find out what cultural events are on in the city, and buy tickets for performances and exhibitions.

LA BOQUERIA

On the right-hand side of the street is one of La Rambla's great attractions: the **Mercat de Sant Josep**, usually called **La Boqueria** ❷ (www.boqueria.info; Mon–Sat 8am–8.30pm). This ornate, 19th-century covered market is a cornucopia of delights for the senses: fresh fish, meats, sausages, fruits and vegetables, all kinds of spices, neatly braided ropes of garlic, sun-dried tomatoes and peppers, preserves and sweetmeats, to make a gourmand swoon. La Boqueria is also a startlingly vibrant community, where shoppers and merchants greet each other by name, ribald sallies across the aisles set off gales of laughter, and the freshness of the *rape* (an angler fish popular in Catalonia) is debated with passion.

The huge market is laid out under high-ceilinged ironwork naves, like a railway station. Restaurants in and near the market are like first-aid stations for those who become faint with hunger. The best time to visit is when practised shoppers and restaurateurs go – early in the morning.

The heart of the Rambla is nearby, at the Pla de la Boqueria, a busy intersection near the Liceu metro station paved with an unmistakable Joan Miró mosaic. Here stands one of Europe's great opera houses, the **Gran Teatre del Liceu** (guided tours daily at 10am, unguided tours daily at 11.30am, noon, 12.30pm and 1pm), inaugurated in 1861. Montserrat Caballé and Josep Carreras made their reputations singing at this theatre, a monument of the Catalan Renaissance and favourite haunt of the Catalan elite. The opera house was gutted by a fire in 1994 (the third it has suffered). After a stunning restoration project

La Boqueria market

that preserved the soul of the historic theatre while adding technological improvements and doubling its size, the Liceu reopened in 1999.

Directly across the Rambla is the Cafè de l'Òpera, a handsome, *modernista*-style café that's always busy and retains a local feel although it is also popular with visitors. It's a good spot for refreshment before you push on down the **Rambla dels Caputxins**. The Rambla's character, like the incline, goes downhill after the Liceu, but the street-entertainment factor rises in inverse proportion. Wade your way through jugglers, human statues, fire-eaters, tarot-card readers, lottery-ticket sellers, hair-braiders and street artists rapidly knocking out portraits, caricatures and chalk master-works on the pavement.

PALAU GÜELL

On the right side of the street is the **Hotel Oriente** (see page 135), which preserves a 17th-century Franciscan convent and cluister inside. Note the naïve painted angels floating over the doorway of what was Ernest Hemingway's favourite Barcelona lodging. Just beyond, on Carrer Nou de la Rambla is **Palau Güell ❸** (www.palauguell.cat; Apr–Sept Tue–Sat 10am–8pm), the mansion that Gaudí (see page 54) built in 1885 for his principal patron, textile tycoon Count Eusebi Güell. Reopened in 2011 following extensive renovation, this extraordinary building is structured around an enormous salon, from which a conical roof covered in mosaic tiles emerges to preside over an unusual landscape of capriciously placed battlements, balustrades and strangely shaped chimneys.

PLAÇA REIAL

Returning to the Rambla, cross over into the arcaded **Plaça Reial**. This handsome, spacious square is graced with a fountain, palm trees, and wrought-iron lamp-posts designed by the young Gaudí. Like the Boqueria market and other landmarks, this square came into being as a result of the destruction of a convent, when church property was expropriated in the mid-19th century. Plaça Reial is a fun and lively place, lined with bars, cafés and restaurants that offer pavement seating, and is buzzing with action night and day. Frequently street entertainers and buskers will pop up to add to the atmosphere.

Mosaic chimney on Palau Güell

Leading down to the harbour is the short **Rambla de Santa Mònica**, beginning at the Plaça del Teatre, site of the Teatre Principal. The warren of alleys to the right,

Plaça Reial

once known as the **Barri Xino**, is still pretty seedy and not the best place for a midnight stroll, but some of the old bars are becoming fashionable again, while the atmospheric Pastís bar has not changed in decades.

Carrer dels Escudellers, a busy pedestrian street on the other side of the Rambla, is the gateway to a district of clubs, bars, restaurants and trendy boutiques, and the delights of the Gothic Quarter. At its far end, Plaça George Orwell has become a trendy place to congregate.

Back on La Rambla, **Arts Santa Mònica** (www.artssanta monica.cat; Tue–Fri 11am–9pm, Sat 11am–2pm, 4–9pm) is an avant-garde contemporary arts centre in a 17th-century convent.

Nearer the port is the **Museu de Cera** ❹ (www.museocera bcn.com; Mon–Fri 10am–1.30pm, 4–7.30pm, Sat–Sun 11am–2pm, 4.30–8.30pm, until 10pm in summer), a tourist trap with 300-plus wax effigies. The Rambla ends at the broad, open space facing the **Mirador de Colom**, a statue honouring Christopher

The Catedral

Columbus where an elevator ascends to the top (temporarily closed at time of writing) for good views of the port. Just beyond lies Barcelona's revitalised waterfront.

BARRI GÒTIC

From its beginnings more than 2,000 years ago, Barcelona has grown outwards in rings, like concentric ripples on a pond. The ancient core is a hill the Romans called Mont Tàber, where they raised a temple to Augustus Caesar and in the 4th century AD built high walls about 1.5km (1 mile) long to protect their settlement. This is the nucleus of the medieval district called the **Barri Gòtic** or Gothic Quarter, with its remarkable concentration of medieval palaces and churches, many built on Roman foundations.

THE CATHEDRAL

The best place to begin a tour is the superb **Catedral** ❺ (Mon–Fri 8am–12.45pm, 5–7.30pm, Sat until 6pm, Sun 8–9am, 5–6pm; charge for some areas), the neighbourhood's focal point. It was begun in 1298 on the site of earlier churches going back to Visigothic times. The final touch – the florid Gothic facade – was not completed until the end of the 19th century and thus contrasts with the simple, octagonal towers. The ribs of the cathedral's high vault are joined at carved and painted keystone medallions, a typically Catalan feature. In the centre of the nave is a splendid Gothic choir with lacy spires.

Steps under the altar lead to the alabaster tomb of Santa Eulàlia, one of the city's two patron saints, martyred in the 4th century and celebrated with a *Festa Major* in February. On the wall of the right aisle are the tombs of Count Ramón Berenguer I and his wife Almodis, who founded the earlier cathedral on this spot in 1058. The Catalan Gothic altarpieces of the Transfiguration painted for the Sant Salvador chapel in the 15th century by Bernat Martorell are considered his masterpiece.

The leafy cloister is a lively refuge, with birds fluttering among the orange, magnolia and palm trees and inhabited by 13 geese, symbolising the age of Eulàlia when she died. Watch where you walk, as the cloister is paved with tombstones, badly worn, but many still bearing the ancient emblems of the boot-makers', tailors' and other craft guilds whose wealth helped pay for the cathedral. From the cloister, pass to the **Capella de Santa Llúcia**, a chapel with 13th- and 14th-century tombstones on the floor and a monu-ment to a crusader knight in armour on one wall.

Thirteen geese live in the cathedral cloister in the National Gallery

Leaving the chapel by its front entrance, turn left into Carrer del Bisbe. Look up as you walk through the old town to take in the details – a curious hanging sign, a lantern, an unusual sculp-ture or plants trailing from balconies. On the right is a row of gargoyles leaning from the roof of the Palau de

The Catedralbar in El Raval

la Generalitat, where there is also a richly ornamented gateway. The lacy overhead bridge is Gothic in style but is actually a 1929 addition.

PLAÇA SANT JAUME

Just ahead is the **Plaça Sant Jaume ❻**, the heart of the Barri Gòtic, where the Government of Catalonia, the Generalitat, faces the Casa de la Ciutat (city hall, also known as the Ajuntament). Though the institutions they house are not always in agreement, the two buildings are a harmonious pair: both have classical facades that hide their Gothic origins. The Generalitat (www.gencat.net) can only be visited on the second and fourth Sunday of the month between 10am and 1.30pm.

The **Palau de la Generalitat**, on the north side of the square, is the more interesting of the two. It dates from 1359, when it was made the executive branch, reporting to the Corts Catalanes (parliament). The nucleus of the present building is the main patio – pure Catalan Gothic, with an open staircase leading to a gallery of arches on slender pillars. The star feature here is the flamboyant Gothic facade of the **Capella de Sant Jordi**. The **Saló de Sant Jordi**, a vaulted hall in the 17th-century front block of the building, is lined with modern murals of historical scenes.

The **Ajuntament** (tel: 934-027 000; tours Sun and some festive days 10am–1.30pm), across the plaza, has held Barcelona's city hall since 1372. It was here that the Consell de Cent, a council of 100 notable citizens, met to deal with civic affairs under the watchful eyes of the king. The original entrance can be seen around the left corner of the building, on the Carrer de la Ciutat. Inside, the left staircase leads to the upper gallery of the old courtyard and to the **Saló de Cent** (Hall of the One Hundred) with a barrel-vaulted ceiling. The red-and-yellow bars of Catalonia's flag decorate the walls. The hall where the city council now meets adjoins, and at the head of the black marble staircase is the **Saló de les Cròniques** (Hall of the Chronicles), noted for the modern murals in sepia tones by Josep Maria Sert.

From behind the Ajuntament, take the short Carrer d'Hèrcules to Plaça Sant Just for a peek at the church of **Sants Just i Pastor** and the pretty little square on which it sits, evocative of a bygone Barcelona. The church is one of the oldest in the city, though it was repeatedly remodelled. It is said that any will sworn before its altar is recognised as valid by the courts of Barcelona, a practice dating from the 10th century.

Nearby on Carrer de la Ciutat is the **Museu d'idees i invents de Barcelona** (miba; www.mibamuseum.com; Mon–Fri 10am–7pm, Sat 10am–8pm, Sun 10am–2pm), a modern museum opened in 2011, dedicated to ideas, inventions and creativity.

September festival

The Plaça Sant Jaume is the meeting place for the giants *(gegants)*, the huge regal figures that process through the streets at the festival of La Mercè, one of Barcelona's patron saints (with Santa Eulàlia), in September. It is also where you will see *castells* – human towers reaching nine people high – an attraction at various fiestas.

PLAÇA DEL REI

From Plaça Sant Just take Dagueria, cross over Jaume I and follow the street up to Baixada Llibreteria, home to one of Barcelona's oldest and tiniest coffee shops, El Mesón del Café. One block down on the left is Veguer, which leads to the **Plaça del Rei** and the **Museu d'Història de la Ciutat de Barcelona** ❼ (MUHBA; City History Museum; Tue–Sun 10am–8pm). The building is a Gothic mansion that was moved stone by stone to this location. In the basement, excavations have uncovered a portion of the Roman city, including shops running along the inside of the Roman wall. Dyeing vats for a clothing industry and evidence of wine-making have been unearthed. Most importantly, however, evidence has been revealed of an early church on the site with a bishop's residence, which provides the link between the Roman and medieval cities. A lift takes visitors down to view the subterranean city.

Above them is the **Palau Reial Major** (Royal Palace) into which you emerge at the end of the excavations. The main buildings here are the chapel, tower and great hall. The **Capella de Santa Àgata** (Chapel of St Agatha) is notable for the 15th-century altarpiece of the *Adoration of the Magi* by one of Catalonia's finest artists, Jaume Huguet. The many-arched Renaissance **Torre de Marti** (Martin the Humanist, last of the dynasty of Barcelona counts) that dominates Plaça del Rei is not currently open to the public.

The vast, barrel-vaulted great hall or throne room, the **Saló del Tinell**, was built for royal audiences in 1359 under Pere III (the Ceremonius) by Guillem Carbonell. On occasion the Corts Catalanes (Parliament) met here. This is where Ferdinand and Isabella supposedly received Columbus in 1493 on his return from his first voyage to the Americas. It was later used as a church, and by the Inquisition, whose victims were burned at the stake in the square. Concerts

Palau Reial Major (Royal Palace)

are held in the square in summer, notably during the La Mercè fiesta.

Behind the Royal Palace, off Carrer Tapineria, is Plaça de Berenguer el Gran, which has a well-preserved section of the original Roman wall. The defences were 9 metres (30ft) high, 3.5 metres (12ft) thick and marked at intervals by towers 18 metres (59ft) tall. Until 1943, most of this section was covered by old houses, which were removed to restore the walls to view.

TOWARDS THE MUSEU FREDERIC MARÈS

A former wing of the palace that encloses the Plaça del Rei was rebuilt in 1557 to become the **Palau del Lloctinent** (Palace of the Lieutenant), residence of the king's representative. It has been beautifully renovated and can now be visited, via an entrance on Carrer dels Comtes. Notice its elegant patio with a noble staircase and remarkable carved wooden ceiling.

Museu Frederic Marès

Just beyond, flanking the cathedral, is the **Museu Frederic Marès** ❽ (www.museumares.bcn.cat; Tue–Sat 10am–7pm, Sun 11am–8pm), which has a beautiful courtyard with an attractive café in the summer months. Marès, a 20th-century sculptor of civic statues, was a compulsive collector who bequeathed to Barcelona an unusually idiosyncratic collection of art and miscellany. The lower floors of the museum house the sculpture collection. The Collector's Cabinet takes up the second and third floors, described as 'a museum within museum'. Recent additions to the cabinet are the Weapons Hall and the Gentlemen's Hall.

ROMAN REMAINS AND THE JEWISH GHETTO

Retracing your steps on the narrow street flanking the cathedral, circle around to the rear and duck into the narrow Carrer del Paradís. Here, just inside the doorway of the Centre Excursionista de Catalunya, four columns of the

Roman Temple of Augustus are embedded in the wall. This narrow lane takes you back into Plaça Sant Jaume. Streets radiate in all directions, each an invitation to explore the Barri Gòtic. The **Carrer del Call** leads into the labyrinth of narrow streets that was the Call, or Jewish Quarter, until the late 14th century. Today the quarter bustles with antiques shops and dealers of rare books, plus bars and restaurants frequented by antiquarians and artists. Just off St Domènec del Call is the **Centre d'Interpretació del Call** (Placeta de Mannel Ribé; Tue–Fri 11am–2pm, Sat–Sun 11am–7pm; free), an information centre on this historic area, with some interesting relics and facts from the period.

Meander into Baixada de Santa Eulàlia. Just off it is tiny **Plaça Sant Felip Neri**, a peaceful square, where the church was pockmarked by Italian bombs during the Civil War. Boutique hotel Neri, in a 17th-century building, has a privileged view of the scene. The **Museu del Calcat** (Museum of the History of Footwear; Tue–Sun 11am–2pm) is at No. 5, once the shoemaker's guild.

EL CALL

Barcelona's Jews, though noted as doctors, scholars and jewellers, were confined to the Call and forced to wear long, hooded cloaks with yellow headbands. Taxation of the community was a source of royal income. This did not save the Call from being burned and looted as persecution of the Jews throughout Spain mounted in the 13th and 14th centuries. Eventually the Jews of Barcelona were killed, expelled or forcibly converted to Christianity, and their synagogues were turned into churches. Just off Carrer del Call, at Carrer de Marlet 1, a medieval inscription in Hebrew marks the site of a hospital founded by one 'Rabbi Samuel Hassareri, may his life never cease'.

Inside Santa Maria del Pi

ANTIQUE ALLEY

The Baixada de Santa Eulàlia descends to **Carrer de Banys Nous**, named for the long-gone 12th-century 'new' baths of the ghetto. This winding street, which more or less follows the line of the old Roman wall, is the unofficial boundary of the Barri Gòtic. It is also known as the Carrer dels Antiquaris – the street of antique dealers. Keep your eyes peeled for unusual hand-painted shop signs, the fretwork of Gothic balconies, and dusty treasures in the shop windows. You will also notice the old tile signs with a cart symbol high on the walls, the indication of one-way streets.

A TRIO OF PLAZAS

Around the corner is a trio of impossibly pretty plazas. **Plaça Sant Josep Oriol** adjoins **Plaça del Pi**, on which sits **Santa Maria del Pi ❾**, a handsome Catalan Gothic church with a tall, octagonal bell tower and a harmonious facade pierced by a large 15th-century rose window. 'Pi' means pine tree, and there is a small one here replacing the landmark specimen of past centuries. Buildings in the plaza show the *sgrafitto* technique of scraping designs in coloured plaster, imported from Italy in the early 1700s. Barcelona's emerging merchant class favoured such facades as an inexpensive substitute for the sculptures on aristocratic palaces.

These adjoining squares, together with the smaller **Placeta del Pi** to the rear of the church, are the essence of old Barcelona and a great place to while away the hours. The bars with tables spread out under leafy trees in each of the squares are magnets for young people and visitors, who are entertained by roving musicians. On Sunday, artists offer their canvases for sale in lively Plaça Sant Josep Oriol, where the Bar del Pi is a popular meeting place. At weekends, a farmers' market selling cheeses, bread and honey is set up in the Plaça del Pi.

The street that leads north from Plaça del Pi, **Carrer Petritxol**, is one of the Barri Gòtic's most traditional. The narrow alley is lined with art galleries, framing shops and traditional *granjas* – good stops for pastries and hot chocolate. Barcelona's oldest and most famous art gallery is **Sala Parés** at No. 5.

Carrer de Banys Nous

AROUND PLAÇA NOVA

At Carrer Portaferrisa, a left turn will take you to La Rambla, while a right turn will take you back to the cathedral and a handful of additional sights on the perimeter of the Barri Gòtic. (You could also return to Plaça Sant

Josep Oriol and take Carrer de la Palla.) In **Plaça Nova**, in front of the cathedral, is the Col.legi d'Arquitectes (Architects' Association). Picasso designed the graffiti-like drawings of the Three Kings and children bearing palm branches that are etched on the 1960s facade. For three weeks in December, a market selling Nativity figures and Christmas trees occupies the Plaça Nova – a square that got its name, 'New', in 1356 and has held markets for nearly 1,000 years. Look for the strange, quintessential Catalan figure, *el caganer* – the red-capped peasant squatting and defecating beside the manger.

The pedestrian thoroughfare that leads north to Plaça de Catalunya is **Avinguda Portal de l'Àngel**, one of the city's main shopping streets, especially busy when *rebaixes* (sales) are on. Look for little Carrer Montsió, which leads to **Els Quatre Gats** (The Four Cats; see page 106), a bar and restaurant that became famous when Picasso and a group of young intellectuals – painters Ramón Casas and Santiago Rusiñol among them – frequented it. Picasso had his first exhibition here in 1901, and the bar, one of the first commissions for the *modernista* architect Puig i Cadafalch, preserves its turn-of-the-20th-century ambience and is, understandably, a great favourite with visitors to Barcelona.

LA RIBERA

Some of the most beautiful Gothic architecture and most fascinating medieval corners of Barcelona lie just outside the Barri Gòtic on the other side of Via Laietana – a traffic-filled avenue roughly parallel to the Ramblas, which was cut through the city in 1859 to link the port with the modern centre (the Eixample). This atmospheric quarter, **La Ribera**, is home to the Museu Picasso and the majestic church of **Santa Maria del Mar** ⑩ (Mon–Sat 9am–1.30pm, 4.30–8pm, Sun 10.30am–1.30pm, 4.30–9pm; free). Carrer de l'Argenteria cuts a diagonal swathe from

Santa Maria del Mar has wonderful acoustics

Plaça de l'Angel to the church. Begun in 1329 at the height of Catalonia's expansion as a Mediterranean power, it is the greatest example of pure Catalan Gothic, with unadorned exterior walls, a sober facade flanked by three-tiered octagonal bell towers, and a beautiful rose window over the portal.

The dimensions and austerity of the interior are breathtaking. Fires during Civil War rioting in 1936 consumed all the trappings of chapels, choir and altar, leaving the interior stripped to its essence. The result is a lofty hall suffused with soft light from the stained-glass windows. Three naves are supported by slim, octagonal columns set 13 metres (43ft) apart, and the dimensions of the interior are multiples of this distance, achieving a perfect symmetry. Behind the simple altar, the columns branch high overhead into the arched vaulting of the apse.

The acoustics are excellent, best demonstrated by the concerts held in the church. Santa Maria is much favoured for weddings so you may find it closed to the public if one is in progress when you arrive.

EL BORN

The rear door of the church leads to the **Passeig del Born**, a pretty, rectangular plaza where jousts were held in the Middle Ages and which today is the nucleus of this fashionable area, full of smart galleries, restaurants, bars and chic shops. Many of the little streets surrounding the church are named after the guilds of the craftsmen who once worked here, such as Sombrerers (Hatmakers), Mirallers (Mirror-makers) and Espasería (Sword-makers). The area is better known now for the people who fill its designer bars late into the night and spill out onto the streets. At the end, the magnificent, wrought-iron **El Born Centre Cultural**, the old fruit-and-vegetable market, has been converted into a museum and cultural centre. It features the archaeological ruins of a medieval city and aims to show how life was in the city from 1713-1714. The centre also hosts concerts and exhibitions.

PABLO PICASSO

The world's most acclaimed 20th-century artist, Pablo Ruiz y Picasso was born in 1881 in Málaga, the son of an art teacher, whose work took the family to Barcelona. Pablo began his art studies here and became part of a group of innovative artists and writers. In 1900, Picasso first visited Paris, and settled there four years later. He never returned to Barcelona after 1934 and, had he wanted to do so, his opposition to the Franco regime would have made it impossible, but his work always retained strong Spanish links. When Picasso died in 1973 (two years before the death of Franco and the end of the dictatorship), the bulk of his own collection, now in the Musée Picasso in Paris, went to the French government in a deal to settle taxes

CARRER MONTCADA AND THE MUSEU PICASSO

One of Barcelona's grandest medieval streets, **Carrer Montcada**, populated by aristocrats from the 14th to the 16th centuries, is lined with splendid Gothic palaces, each with an imposing door or arched gate to an inner courtyard from where an ornamental staircase usually led up to reception rooms. These mansions were gradually abandoned after the demolition of the adjoining district and construction of the Ciutadella fortress. This quarter is the most authentically medieval part of the city.

Museu Picasso

The **Museu Picasso ⑪** (www.museupicasso.bcn.es; Tue–Sun 10am–8pm), occupies five palaces (two used for temporary exhibitions). The main entrance is through the 15th-century **Palau Aguilar**. The buildings were acquired by the city to house the collection of paintings, drawings and ceramics donated by Picasso's lifelong friend and secretary, Jaume Sabartés. After the museum opened in 1963, Picasso added sketches and paintings from his childhood and youth. The earliest works date from his ninth year. As a teenager he produced large canvases in the 19th-century realist style, such as the *First Communion* and *Science and Charity*. It appears that, as Picasso's talent developed, he digested the styles of the past and of his contemporaries, proved he could equal them, then forged ahead.

The collection of his work is the largest outside Paris, and while it doesn't possess any of his finest pieces, it does have two good examples of his Blue Period (1901–4), as well as *The*

Harlequin (1917), and the idiosyncratic *Las Meninas* series, the variations on the theme of the Velázquez masterpiece in Madrid's Prado Museum, which provides a fascinating view of Picasso's innovative and deconstructivist approach to his subject. Alongside the existing exhibition halls is a new building housing a research centre.

Opposite, down Barra de Fero, the **Museu Europa d'Art Modern** (MEAM; www.meam.es; Tue–Sat 10am–8pm) is a recent acquisition that promotes figurative art from the late 19th century to the present day.

MORE MANSIONS AND MUSEUMS

The **Museu del Disseny** (Disseny Hub Barcelona; Tue–Sun 10am 8pm, free admission Sun from 3 8pm and the first Sun of the month), is a centre that merges design museums, research and production. This hub contains three DHUB museums housed under one roof in the much-vaunted Design Museum in Plaça de les Glòries. Regular exhibitions take place and permanent collections include fashion, textiles, product design and decorative arts.

Situated within a 16th-century palace, the **Museu Barbier-Mueller** (Montcada 14; Tue–Fri 11am–7pm, Sat–Sun 11am–8pm) showcases a collection of pre-Columbian art. All the mansions along here merit a peek in at the courtyards, but one that's always open is the handsome, baroque **Palau Dalmases** (No. 20). On the ground floor is Espai Barroc (Baroque Space), an over-the-top, rococo bar. At the end of the street, in Plaçeta Montcada, you can get wonderful Basque tapas in the Euskal Etxea bar (see page 107).

PALAU DE LA MÚSICA

Up Via Laietana several blocks from Carrer Princesa, at Carrer del Palau de la Música 4–6, is one of the city's greatest

Stunning Palau de la Música Catalana

achievements of *modernista* architecture, the **Palau de la Música Catalana** (www.palaumusica.org; guided tours daily 10am–3.30pm, Aug until 6pm, booking advised). Designed by Lluís Domènech i Montaner, and inaugurated in 1908, it is the perfect expression of *modernisme* and has been designated a Unesco World Heritage Site. Recently expanded, it is an explosion of mosaics, tiles, stained glass, enamel, sculpture and carving. The brick exterior, with Moorish arches and columns inlaid with floral tiles, is sober compared to what's inside, where every square inch is embellished.

One of Domènech's main concerns was to let in as much natural light as possible, making the hall light and roomy. The structural skeleton is iron – an innovation in those days – which allows the walls to be made of glass. Sunlight streaming in during afternoon concerts sets the place on fire. On either side of the stage the rich colours of the room are offset by sculpted groups of musical masters in white plaster. Between them,

Casa Lleó Morera on Passeig de Gràcia

the silvery pipes of a grand organ stand in orderly contrast. A curved wall is covered with mosaics of muses playing instruments; their upper bodies are made of porcelain and seem to emerge magically from the walls. Overhead is the Palau's crowning glory, a magical, stained-glass orb.

The best way to experience the Palau is to attend a concert. Programmes range from classical recitals to jazz (box office tel: 902 442 882; Sept–June 9.30am–3.30pm, July–Aug 9am–9pm). The alleyways opposite lead to Santa Caterina market, a dazzling renovation by architects EMTB, creators of the Scottish Parliament building, and a great place to eat.

EL EIXAMPLE

The **Eixample** district, north of Plaça de Catalunya, is the city's main shopping and commercial area. You will probably want to spend a lot of time here if you are interested in Gaudí. The neighbourhood has spectacular apartment blocks, examples of early 20th-century *modernista* architecture, and the central part is known as the **Quadrat d'Or** (Golden Square).

The principal avenues are the elegant Passeig de Gràcia and the Rambla de Catalunya, not to be confused with the Rambles in the Old Town. In a manageable area between the Gran Vía de les Corts Catalanes and Avinguda Diagonal, you'll find most of the *modernista* masterpieces. Barcelona's most visited sight is Gaudí's unfinished cathedral La Sagrada Família: on the northern outskirts of the Eixample, it can be easily reached on foot or by metro.

Despite the exuberance of the architecture, the city's 'modern' district is a model of rationalist urban planning, a rigid geometric grid simply called 'the Extension' *(Eixample)*. The outrageous and conservative coexist here without much fuss. Barcelona's expansion came about in a remarkable burst of urban development. By the mid-1800s the city was bursting at the seams and suffocating inside its ring of medieval walls. A competition was held in 1859 to select a plan for a new quarter between the old city and the Collserola hills. The job went to an engineer named Ildefons Cerdà, whose plan quintupled the city's size in a matter of decades. The Eixample construction transformed Barcelona into a showcase of extravagant *modernista* architecture, and the swanky Passeig de Gràcia became the place to be seen. Barcelona used the 1888 Universal Exposition as an open house to show the world its new face.

THE ILLA DE LA DISCÒRDIA

The best place to begin a *modernista* tour is on Passeig de Gràcia, with its single, hallucinatory block popularly known as the **Illa de la Discòrdia** ⑬ (Block of Discord), set between Consell de Cent and Aragó. It gained its name because of the three stunning buildings in markedly different architectural

Casa Batlló

styles that are located almost next door to each other.

At No. 35 Domènech i Montaner's impressive **Casa Lleó Morera** (1902–6) incorporates both Moorish and Gothic elements. This grand apartment house has suffered some disfigurement, especially on the ground floor, where the Spanish leather goods company Loewe installed picture windows and destroyed several original sculptures. The building now contains offices and sadly cannot be visited.

At No. 41 is the **Casa Amatller** (1900), which was built for a chocolate manufacturer. Puig i Cadafalch drew inspiration from Flanders for the stepped roof covered in glazed tiles. The ground-floor entrance is open to visitors (free), where the caretaker's office contains one of the finest stained-glass windows of the *modernista* era. There is also a gallery displaying temporary exhibitions.

CASA BATLLÓ

Gaudí's highly personal **Casa Batlló** (1904–6) is next door and can now be visited, to the delight of many (www.casabatllo.es; daily 9am–8pm, book online as there can be a queue). The curvy contours, unexpected combinations of textures and materials, bright colours and infinite detail are Gaudí hallmarks, as are the prevalent religious and nationalist symbols. Casa Batlló is said to pay tribute to the patron saint of Catalonia, Sant Jordi, and the dragon he slayed. Gaudí himself left no clues as to his intent. The undulating blue-tile roof certainly looks like a dragon's scaly hide, while the balconies could be the skulls and bones of its victims (others have suggested they are Venetian carnival masks). Sant Jordi's cross and a shaft suggest a spear being thrust into the dragon's back. Casa Batlló's facade is covered with scraps of broken plate and tile, a decorative technique called *trencadís* that Gaudí employed repeatedly. In this case he dramatically remodelled both the exterior and interior of an existing house.

LA PEDRERA

Further up and across the street, at No. 92, is **Casa Milà ⓮** (tel: 934 845 900; www.pedrera.com; daily, Mar–Oct 10am–8pm, Nov–Feb 9am–6.30pm), Gaudí's acclaimed apartment block. Known as **La Pedrera** (the Quarry, an allusion to its rippling, limestone surface), it was built between 1906 and 1910, and has been declared a Unesco World Heritage Site. The sinuous facade, with wonderfully twisted wrought-iron balconies, bends around the corner of Carrer Provença. It was given a

MODERNISME

Modernisme, a movement related to the design styles in vogue in Europe in the late 19th century – French Art Nouveau, German and Austrian Jugendstil – was a rebellion against the rigid forms and colourless stone and plaster of classical architecture. In Barcelona the new style assumed nationalist motifs and significance, which may be why it has been so carefully preserved here. Although there was an entire school of modernista architects working in Barcelona from the late 19th century until the 1930s, it is customary to speak of the 'Big Three': Antoni Gaudí, who left such a personal mark on the city; Lluís Domènech i Montaner (Palau de la Música Catalana and Casa Morera); and Josep Puig i Cadafalch (Casa Amatller, Casa Terrades and Els Quatre Gats), all of which are described in this guide.

Sinuous facade of Casa Milà

facelift in the mid-1990s, and it looks better than ever. The apartments inside had suffered unspeakable horrors, and Gaudí's beautiful arched attics were sealed up, but today everything has been restored to its original state.

The attic floor is now a handsome, high-tech museum (Espai Gaudí) with an interesting exhibition of his work. One of the original apartments (El Pis), all odd shapes, hand-crafted door knobs, and idiosyncratic details, has been outfitted with period furniture (many of the pieces designed by Gaudí himself), and can be visited.

La Pedrera had one of the world's first underground parking garages; today the space houses an amphitheatre where cultural conferences are held. The building's owner, the cultural Fundació Caixa de Catalunya, has transformed the first floor into an exhibition space for impressively curated shows.

For many, the wavy rooftop is the highlight, with its decoration of recycled tiles, cluster of swirling Darth Vader-like chimneys, known as 'witch scarers' and spectacular views of Barcelona.

PASSEIG DE GRÀCIA

You are likely to be busy looking up at decorative details or gazing in chic store windows along **Passeig de Gràcia**, but be sure to notice the ground as well: Gaudí designed the hexagonal pavement tiles with nature motifs. The mosaic benches and iron street lamps with little bat motifs (1900) are by Pere Falqués.

There are other numerous examples of *modernisme* throughout the Eixample. Have a look at the streets which cut across Passeig de Gràcia, especially Diputació, Consell de Cent, Mallorca and València. In the old town you'll stumble across marvellous *modernista* store fronts, such as the stamp shop at Carrer dels Boters, the Antiga Casa Figueras pastry shop on the Ramblas and the wonderful dining room of the Hotel España in Carrer Sant Pau. In addition, details of a special route, the Ruta del Modernisme, which visits at least 115 examples, can be found online at www.rutadelmodernisme.com. A guidebook is also available that gives discounts on entrance tickets.

If Barcelona's given you the design bug, the excellent shop **Vinçon**, at Passeig de Gràcia 96, specialises in design. It's well worth a visit, for its inspiring contents and for the spectacular turn-of-the-20th-century palace it is housed in. You can explore the mansion that once belonged to Picasso's contemporary, the painter Ramón Casas, whilst finding out how design-conscious Barceloneses decorate their homes.

Inside the design shop Vinçon

In addition to the jewels of *modernista* architecture, Passeig de Gràcia and neighbouring Rambla Catalunya are lined with cafés, galleries, bookstores, elegant fashion boutiques and smart hotels. This is definitely the place for designer shopping, for both international and top Spanish names like Adolfo

Dominguez and Catalans Antonio Miró and Armand Basi, as well as more down-to-earth fashion, such as that at Zara, the Spanish enterprise that has now become internationally known for inexpensive, young fashion.

AROUND THE AVENUES

The **Plaça de Catalunya**, where Passeig de Gràcia begins, was designed to be the city's hub, and it is certainly a lively crossroads and meeting place, especially the legendary Café Zurich. The bus, metro, and the regional and national rail systems radiate from this square (see Transport, page 130) and El Corte Inglés department store occupies the whole of the northern side.

Parallel to Passeig de Gràcia is the Rambla de Catalunya, an extension of the Old Town Rambles, lined with smart shops, terrace cafés, restaurants and galleries. Traffic moves down either side, but the centre is pedestrian-only and is considerably more sedate than the lower Rambles.

ANTONI GAUDÍ

Count Eusebi Güell, a textile manufacturer, was Gaudí's patient and daring patron, a man who was able to accept the architect's wildly imaginative ideas. The Palau Güell, which Gaudí began in 1885 (see page 29), previews many aspects of his work. Gaudí died in 1926 at the age of 74, and is buried in the crypt of his great cathedral.

He was a deeply pious and conservative man, despite his innovations, and during his last years he lived in a room on the site, obsessed with the project. When passers-by discovered the architect run over by a tram in a nearby street in 1926 and took him to hospital, the doctors, unable at first to identify him, thought the dishevelled old man was a tramp. When it was discovered who he was, the entire city turned out for his funeral

On Carrer d'Aragó (between Passeig de Gràcia and Rambla Catalunya) is the **Fundació Antoni Tàpies**  (www.fundaciotapies.org; Tue–Sun 10am–7pm), dedicated to the work of Catalonia – and perhaps Spain's – foremost contemporary artist (1923–2012). Recently reopened following major renovation, in addition to Tàpies' own work, it holds excellent temporary exhibitions, a study centre and library, and it is all housed in a gorgeous 1880 Domènech i Montaner building – one of the first examples of *modernisme*. From the outside, viewed from across the street,

Sagrada Família's central nave

you can appreciate Tàpies' whimsical, tangled wire sculpture *Núvol i Cadira* (Cloud and Chair) on the roof.

LA SAGRADA FAMÍLIA

What the Eiffel Tower is to Paris or the Statue of Liberty is to New York, the soaring spires of the **Sagrada Família**  (www.sagradafamilia.org; daily Apr–Sept 9am–8pm, Oct–Mar 9am–6pm) are to Barcelona. Its unmistakable profile, protruding from the city's skyline, is visible from afar. Yet the eight peculiar, cigar-shaped towers are merely the shell of a church that is still many years from completion, though its progress has accelerated in recent years. This was Antoni Gaudí's life work, though he didn't really expect to finish it in his lifetime. Gaudí took over traditional, neo-Gothic plans of an earlier architect in 1883 and supervised work on the eastern, Nacimiento (Nativity) facade, one tower, and part of the apse and nave. This facade seems to be the one most faithful to Gaudí's intentions.

Everything has significance and no space is left unfilled. The three doorways, with stonework dripping like stalactites, represent Faith, Hope and Charity, and are loaded with sculptures depicting angel choirs, musicians and Biblical episodes such as the birth of Jesus, the Flight into Egypt, the Slaughter of the Innocents, the Tree of Calvary, and much more. Twelve bell towers, four at each portal, will represent the Apostles; four higher towers, the Evangelists; a dome over the apse the Virgin; and the central spire, which will be 170 metres (560ft) high, the Saviour.

For many years, the church remained much as it was when Gaudí died, but work has been going on since the 1950s – not an easy task, since Gaudí left few plans behind. Ascend one of the towers (by lift or spiral staircase) for an overview. The western Pasión facade (on Carrer de Sardenya), begun in 1952, includes controversial sculptures by Josep Maria Subirachs. Japanese sculptor Etsuro Sotoo's work can be seen on the Nacimiento facade.

Many people believe the temple should have been left as it was, unfinished, as a tribute to the great Gaudí, but the work continues, supervised by Jordi Bonet Armengol, the son of one of Gaudí's aides. In 2010 the central nave was finally covered, resplendent with its tree-like columns and dazzling roof, but final completion has been moved back to 2030. On 7 November 2010 the church was consecrated by Pope Benedict XVI.

A short walk along Avinguda de Gaudí is the **Hospital de la Santa Creu i Sant Pau** (www.santpau.es; guided tours daily 10am, 11am, noon and 1pm) designed by Domènech i Montaner. A working hospital until 2009, it is one of *modernisme*'s most underrated and least-known works and well worth visiting. A

Park Güell

World Heritage Site, it will now house part of the UN University and become an international centre for the Mediterranean.

GRÀCIA AND PARK GÜELL

Gràcia is a district above the Eixample, retaining a village atmosphere with small local shops and its own town square, Plaça de la Vila de Gràcia (formerly Plaça Rius i Taulet). Streets named Llibertat and Fraternitat and a Plaça Revolució reflect a political past. Gràcia is a popular nightspot, known for its *Festa Major*, which runs for eight days around 15 August. On the hills behind Gràcia, **Park Güell** ⑰ (daily 10am–sunset; free, except for Casa-Museu Gaudí), another wildly ambitious Gaudí project, was planned as a residential community, to be intertwined with nature. Gaudí's patron Eusebi Güell bought 6 hectares (15 acres) here, overlooking the city and the sea, intending to create a kind of English garden suburb. He gave Gaudí carte blanche to produce something original, and for the

Nightfall over Port Vell

next 14 years, on and off, the architect let his imagination run wild, much of the design was, however, eventually completed by Josep Maria Jujol.

Two gingerbread pavilions guard the entrance on Carrer d'Olot: the one on the left is a shop, the one on the right an exhibition centre. In front of them is a tiled lizard fountain; supporting columns mimic tree trunks. Ceilings are decorated with fragments of plates, and undulating benches are splashed with colourful ceramic pieces, known as *trencadís*. Beneath the plaza with the benches is the **Saló de les Cent Columnes** (Hall of the One Hundred Columns). There are actually 86, Doric in style, in what was to be the colony's covered market. Dolls' heads, bottles, glasses and plates are stuck in the ceiling mosaics. Only five buildings were completed, one of which Gaudí lived in for many years, now the **Casa-Museu Gaudí** (daily Apr–Sept 10am–7.45pm, Oct–Mar 10am–5.45pm), a museum of his furniture and memorabilia.

THE WATERFRONT

Barcelona turned its back on the sea during the 19th century and focused on developing industry. The sea wall where families loved to walk and catch the breeze on stifling summer nights was dismantled. Access to the sea was obstructed by warehouses and railway tracks and expansion proceeded towards the hills. Barceloneta, a neighbourhood created in the early 18th century between the port and the beach as part of a military initiative, remained a close-knit working-class community. However, things changed with the creation of an ambitious recreational and commercial area along the waterfront in the early 1990s.

MARITIME HERITAGE

Begin a tour of the waterfront at the Columbus Monument, at the foot of the Ramblas. To the right is **Les Reials Drassanes**, begun in 1255, and now housing the **Museu Marítim 18** (www. mmb.cat; daily 10am–8pm). The 16 bays of these great shipyards, which handled more than 30 galleys, launched ships that extended Catalonia's dominion over the Mediterranean from Tunis to Greece, Sicily, Sardinia and much of the French coast. The museum contains models from the earliest galleys to the cargo and passenger vessels that have made Barcelona their home port. The prize exhibit is a full-size copy of Don Juan of Austria's victorious flagship *La Galera Reial*. The permanent exhibits are not on view at present while the museum is being remodelled, but temporary

The Swallows

A perennial waterfront attraction are the ferries called Golondrinas (Swallows; www.lasgolondrinas.com), moored opposite the Columbus Monument. These boats have been taking passengers round the harbour ever since the 1888 World Exposition.

Shark tunnel in L'Aquàrium

displays are open to the public. The new, more interactive museum is expected to open in 2013.

PORT VELL

At the other side of the busy Passeig de Colom is an undulating wooden walkway and footbridge called the **Rambla del Mar,** which stretches across the mouth of the **Port Vell**. It crosses over to the Moll d'Espanya and **Maremàgnum**, a commercial centre with plenty of shops, bars and restaurants – some with terraces which are a great place to sit and watch the harbour activity. Families head for **L'Aquàrium** ❿ (www.aquariumbcn.com; daily July–Aug 9.30am–11pm, Sept–June 9.30am–9/9.30pm); one of Europe's largest aquariums, with a spectacular glass tunnel running through its huge Oceanarium. Alongside is an Imax 3D cinema.

The port is busy with yachts, cruise ships and ferries to Mallorca and Italy. Overhead, cable cars link Montjuïc with the Torre de Jaume I and the Torre de Sant Sebastià in Barceloneta. The **World Trade Center**, a hotel and complex of offices designed by I.M. Pei, appears to be floating in the harbour.

On the mainland, the **Moll de la Fusta**, the old wood-loading quay, was transformed into a broad promenade in the 1980s, and redesigned and landscaped after the 1992 Olympics. Where the Moll d'Espanya joins the promenade stands Roy Lichtenstein's colourful Pop Art sculpture, called the **Barcelona Head** *(Cap de Barcelona)*.

Heading towards Barceloneta you skirt the **Marina Port Vell**, a harbour for luxury yachts and chic motor cruisers. On the **Moll de Barceloneta**, in a stylishly renovated warehouse complex, the Palau de Mar houses the **Museu d'Història de Catalunya ⑳** (www.mhcat.net; Tue–Sat 10am–7pm, Wed until 8pm, Sun 10am–2.30pm), which is fun as well as informative. A restaurant with a stunning view is on the top floor. Along the Passeig Joan de Borbó, which runs parallel to the quay, numerous popular restaurants have outside tables.

BARCELONETA

If you want to eat really good fish, head to Barceloneta, an area for many years separated from the city in spirit as well as by physical barriers of water and rail yards. It was built in the early 18th century to house dispossessed families when La Ribera district was demolished to make way for the Ciutadella fortress. A robust *barrio* inhabited by fishermen's families, its beaches were scruffy and dominated by flimsy wooden restaurant shacks *(chiringuitos)*.

When the area was virtually rebuilt in preparation for the 1992 Olympics, they were wiped out, and many Barceloneses nostalgically

On Carrer Salvador Espriu in the Vila Olímpica

mourn their loss. You can cut through the grid of narrow streets or walk along the beach to the **Passeig Marítim** and the landscaped promenade running alongside the wooden walkways and scrupulously clean sands of **Platja Barceloneta**. Several modern *chiringuitos* and some good restaurants have now opened on the beach, a popular hangout on summer nights.

OLYMPIC VILLAGE AND BEYOND

Keep walking and you will come to the 1992 Olympic Village, the **Vila Olímpica**, an award-winning development that has blossomed into a smart and vibrant neighbourhood. It is recognisable from afar by two high-rise buildings – one the prestigious Hotel Arts – and Frank Gehry's enormous, shimmering copper fish. As you approach, passing a small park, the gleaming Hospital de Mar and a *modernista* water tower, the promenade here and in the **Port Olímpic** just beyond becomes increasingly lined with bars and restaurants.

Beyond the Olympic Port a line of metal poles follow a path inland to the Poble Nou district, known for its textile production. Today the factories have been replaced by design studios, office blocks and apartments, and gentrification continues, spreading north and west to meet Avinguda Diagonal.

At the end of the seafront promenade, **Diagonal Mar** and the Parc del Fòrum have formed a hi-tech residential and commercial neighbourhood. The Universal Forum of Cultures was held here on an esplanade jutting out to sea, and is now a venue for music festivals and conventions. In 2011, the landmark triangular Forum Building became home to the **Museu Blau ㉑** (Blue Museum; www.museuzoologia.bcn.es; Tue–Sun 10am–8pm), an interactive natural history and science museum.

Rebecca Horn's L'Estel Ferit (Wounded Star) pays homage to Barceloneta's old beach restaurants

PARC DE LA CIUTADELLA

Lodged between the Olympic Village and La Ribera is **Parc de la Ciutadella ㉒** the city's largest park, which incorporates the zoo, the **Parc Zoológic** (www.zoobarcelona.cat; daily Apr–Sept 10am–7pm, Mar and Oct 10am–6pm, Nov–Feb 10am–5pm). This was the site, first, of the fortress built after the fall of Barcelona in 1714, and then of the 1888 World Exposition. Housed in a splendid *modernista* building designed for this event is the Laboratori de Natura, housing the zoological collection of the Museu de Ciènces Naturals (www.museuciences.bcn.cat). Under the same umbrella stands the nearby Museu Martorell, which houses the geological collection.

The popular park is always a relaxing refuge from the intensity of the city's streets. It's a lovely place, with a lake where rowing boats can be hired, and shady benches

Madonna sculpture on Mare de Déu de la Mercè

beneath towering trees where parakeets have taken control. The large baroque fountain, **La Cascada**, was designed by Josep Fontseré, whose assistant was a young architecture student named Antoni Gaudí. In the Plaça d'Armes is the Parlament de Catalunya. The autonomous government debates the issues of the day in a handsome building, once the arsenal of the 18th-century citadel.

From the park's exit on Pujades a broad promenade sweeps up to the impossing **Arc de Triomf**, built as the entrance to the 1888 Exposition. To the right, near university buildings on Wellington, a tram can be caught to Diagonal Mar. On the sea side of the park lies the grand Estació de França railway station, and along Avingunda Marquès de l'Argentera is **La Llotja**, a centre of Barcelona's trading activities for more than 600 years and former Stock Exchange. It is a handsome building with an attractive courtyard and a 14th-century Gothic hall.

Almost opposite is the splendid arcade of **Porxos Xifré**, a 19th-century complex that houses the **Restaurant 7 Portes**, a Barcelona institution (see page 111). If you head back towards the Rambla past the city's monumental Correus (Post Office), along Passeig de Colom, you will pass the baroque splendour of the **Mare de Déu de la Mercè** church. It is best known because the sculpture of the Madonna on the dome can be seen for miles around and is something of a local landmark.

EL RAVAL

The district between La Rambla, the Ronda de Sant Antoni and Paral.lel is **El Raval**, where numerous buildings have been demolished to create urban spaces and new housing in the latest trendy zone. From La Rambla, take Carrer del Carme, then turn right up Carrer dels Àngels to reach the most conspicuous symbol of this neighbourhood's transformation: Richard Meier's **Museu d'Art Contemporani de Barcelona ㉓** (MACBA; www.macba.es; Mon, Wed–Fri 11am–7.30pm, Thur until midnight in summer, Sat 10am–8pm, Sun 10am–3pm), which is worth visiting for its architecture and the multicultural buzz in its square, where skateboarders, art lovers and locals all congregate. It has some fine abstract works and good temporary exhibitions.

Next door is the ever-stimulating **Centre de Cultura Contemporània de Barcelona** (CCCB; www.cccb.org; Tue–Sun 11am–8pm), a striking renovation of an old poor house, the Casa de Caritat. In this exciting space dance, music, film and other activities explore the urban experience.

Retrace your steps to Carrer del Carme and the Gothic complex of the **Antic Hospital de la Santa Creu** (Hospital of the Holy Cross), a hospital and refuge for pilgrims for a thousand years. Gaudí died here in 1926. The present structures were begun in 1401. Look for the frieze of 16th-century tiles on the life of St Paul in the entryway of the Institut d'Estudis Catalans. The courtyard is restful, with benches under orange trees ripe with fruit or fragrant with blossom. The Massana Art School and the Library of Catalonia are both housed here.

The sleek modern art gallery MACBA

URBAN REGENERATION

Carrer Hospital is a busy commercial street catering primarily to the Arab and Asian families living in the area. On and around it are some trendy little shops and restaurants, although the narrow alleys are best avoided. Check out Rieva Baixa for vintage shops, and the recently created Rambla del Raval. Old housing was demolished to make way for it, and new blocks and a towering 5-star hotel are all part of the urban regeneration process that is attracting a bohemian crowd.

Around the corner is a Romanesque gem, the little church of **Sant Pau del Camp** (Mon–Sat 10am–1.30pm, 4–7pm, free). The simplicity of its 12th-century lines is an agreeable change from the extravagance of Barcelona's *modernismo* and the intricacies of Gothic architecture. It is believed to be the oldest church in the city. The lovely little cloister has curious, Arab-style arches.

MONTJUÏC

Montjuïc came into its own as the site of Barcelona's 1929 International Exhibition, and again for the 1992 Olympic Games. It has since been rejuvenated so its shady gardens, 210-metre (689ft) summit, panoramic views and outstanding complex of museums and sports facilities are more popular than ever. The Plaça d'Espanya is a good point to begin a visit to Montjuïc, as it has a metro and bus stop. Beside the square is a bullring built in 1899, now home to the **Arenas de Barcelona**, a shopping, cultural and recreational facility. A central avenue leads upwards to the vast **Palau Nacional**, which houses the Catalan art museum, MNAC, and past the **Font Màgica** (Magic Fountain) **24**, which performs a *son et lumière* show (May–Sept Thur–Sun 9–11.30pm, Oct–Apr Fri–Sat 7–9pm). Nearby is the seminal **Pavelló Mies van der Rohe** (www.miesbcn.com; daily 10am– 8pm), built for the 1929 Exposition, dismantled, then rebuilt in 1986. The glass, stone and steel cube house is a wonder of cool Bauhaus forms.

Opposite is **Casaramona**, a magnificent *modernista* textile factory converted into the **CaixaForum** (daily 10am–8pm), the Fundació la Caixa's wonderful cultural centre, with a full programme of exhibitions and concerts.

Font Màgica during a *son et lumière* show

CATALAN ART TREASURES

External elevators make the ascent to the domed Palau Nacional easier. This

Gazing up into the dome of the Palau Nacional

is the **Museu Nacional d'Art de Catalunya ㉕** (MNAC; www.
mnac.cat; Tue–Sat 10am–7pm, Sun 10am–2.30pm), housing
one of the world's finest collections of Romanesque art. It
holds 1,000 years of Catalan art, bringing together various
collections under one roof, including part of the Thyssen-
Bornemisza collection, and the 19th- and 20th-century collection of the former Museu d'Art Modern de Catalunya. It
also holds excellent temporary exhibitions.

Between the 9th and 13th centuries, over 2,000 Romanesque churches were built in Catalonia. Interiors were decorated with painted altar panels, carved wooden crosses,
Madonnas of great purity and primitive sculptures of biblical episodes or rural life on the capitals of columns. At the
start of the 20th century many works were saved from dete-
riorating in abandoned churches and are now housed in the
museum. There are masterpieces in every room. The Gothic
wing is excellent, too. Many of the paintings are retablos,

screens with arched frames that stood behind chapel altars. Among the treasures are Lluís Dalmau's painting *Virgin of the Councillors* (1445); Jaume Ferrer II's altarpiece St Jerome; and a fine retable of St John the Baptist with saints Sebastian and Nicholas.

The 19th- and 20th-century collection includes works by Casas, Fortuny, Mir, Nonell and Rusiñol. Displays have been further enhanced with a collection of paintings from Barcelona-born Carmen Thyssen-Bornemisza.

MUSEUMS AND MIRÓ

Up the hill is the **Museu d'Arqueologia de Catalunya** ㉖ (www.mac.cat; Tue–Sat 9.30am–7pm, Sun 10am–2.30pm). Among the exhibits, drawn mainly from prehistoric, Iberian, Greek and Roman sites in Catalonia, are reconstructions of tombs and life-like dioramas. Around another curve, within walking distance uphill, is the **Museu Etnològic**, highlighting the native arts of Latin America.

Further up lie the Jardins de Laribal, and on the edge of them is the **Teatre Grec** amphitheatre, where the Festival Grec is held in summer. Steps from here lead to the simple and elegant **Fundació Joan Miró** ㉗ (www.fundaciomiro-bcn.org; Tue–Sat 10am–7pm, Thur until 9.30pm, Sun 10am–2.30pm). This excellent museum, which opened in 1975, was

Cable cars

A funicular from Avinguda del Paral.lel metro station runs to Avinguda de Miramar (near the Fundació Joan Miró), and links up with the Telefèric (daily 10am–9pm, shorter hours in winter), the cable car that gives a ride with a view up to the Castell de Montjuïc. Another cable car, the Transbordador Aéri, runs from Montjuïc right across the port to Barceloneta (daily 11am–7/8pm, shorter hours in winter), stopping at the World Trade Center.

designed by the architect Josep Lluís Sert to house a large collection of paintings, drawings, tapestries and sculpture by the Catalan surrealist, who died in 1983 at the age of 90. The exhibits follow Miró's artistic development from 1914 onwards. Flooded with natural light, they are seen at their best. In the grounds outside are a number of his sculptures. The collection is witty and bright with the unique language symbols associated with the artist.

The **Castell de Montjuïc** (daily 9am–7pm, until 9pm in summer; free), built in 1640, remained in use by the army, then as a prison until shortly before it was turned over to the city in 1960. The fort has sombre associations for the city: its cannons bombarded the population to crush rebellions in the 18th and 19th centuries, and it was the site of political executions. The castle can be visited but plans for its future include an International Centre for Peace.

Miró sculpture outside the Fundació

The **Jardí Botànic** (www.museuciencies.bcn.cat; daily 1–5/6pm, July–Aug until 8pm), between the Olympic Stadium and the castle, is a sustainable garden showcasing plants from across the Mediterranean.

The **Anella Olímpica** (Olympic Ring) spreads across the northern side of Montjuïc and can be reached by an

escalator from the Palau Nacional. The original 1929 Estadi Olímpic (Olympic stadium) was enlarged for the 1992 Games and further alterations made for the European Athletics Championships in 2010. Near its entrance is the new **Museu Olímpic i de l'Esport** ㉘ (www. museuolimpicbcn.cat; Tue–Sat 10am–8pm, Oct–Mar until 6pm, Sun 10am–2.30pm), a must for sports enthusiasts.

Torre de Calatrava

Just beyond is the high-tech **Palau Sant Jordi** sports stadium, designed by Japanese architect Arata Isozaki. It can seat 17,000 under a roof 45 metres (148ft) high. Towering over it all is the 188-meter (616ft) -high **Torre de Calatrava** communications tower.

POBLE ESPANYOL

Down the hill is the **Poble Espanyol** ㉙ (Spanish Village; www. poble-espanyol.com; Mon 9am–8pm, Tue–Thur, Sun 9am–midnight, Fri 9am–3am, Sat 9am–4am), a family attraction by day and a popular nightspot. Built for the 1929 Exposition, it's a composite of architecture representing Spain's varied regions, including replicas of houses, church towers, fountains, plazas and palaces arranged along a network of streets and squares. The entrance is through a gate of the walled city of Ávila. There is a flamenco show, restaurants, discos and demonstrations of regional crafts, including weaving, pottery and glass-blowing, which make it a good place to find well-made souvenirs.

Teatre Nacional de Catalunya

THE DIAGONAL

The broad Avinguda Diagonal slices across Cerdà's grid from the coast to the hills linking up with the city ring roads. From Diagonal Mar a tram runs through the newly transformed **22@ district** ㉚ with its cutting-edge architecture up to the busy Plaça de les Glòries Catalanes roundabout. Jean Nouvel's gherkin-like **Torre Agbar**, an office block, spectacularly marks the spot. A huge urban development centred on this square will incorporate DHUB's state-of-the-art premises, expected to open 2013, which will house museums currently in the Palau de Pedralbes (see below). Nearby is Ricardo Bofill's neoclassical **Teatre Nacional de Catalunya** and Rafael Moneo's **L'Auditori**, a concert hall which now includes the **Museu de la Música** (www.bcn.es/museumusica; Mon, Wed–Sat 10am–6pm, Sun 10am–8pm).

PEDRALBES

Further up the Diagonal is the **Palau de Pedralbes**, a Güell-family estate converted into a royal residence in 1919. It houses four museums: the Museu de Ceràmica, Museu de les Arts Decoratives, Museu Tèxtil i d'Indumentària and Gabinet de les Arts Gràfiques, all part of the DHUB (www.dhub-bcn.cat) initiative that will be moved to Les Glòries in 2013 (see above). On the other side of the Diagonal is the Zona Universitària and **Camp Nou Stadium**, home of Barcelona's revered football club, Barça, with a museum which includes a tour (Mon–Sat 10am–8pm, Sun until 2.30pm, with exceptions).

At the top of Avinguda de Pedralbes is the atmospheric **Monestir de Pedralbes** ⑪ (Tue–Fri 10am–5pm, Sat 10am–7pm, Sun 10am–8pm; shorter hours in winter). Founded in 1326 by Queen Elisenda de Montcada, whose tomb is in the superb Gothic church, it has a beautiful three-storey cloister.

The districts on the hillsides were once separate villages where residents of Barcelona spent summers and weekends. They've been absorbed over the years, but each preserves its own character. Pedralbes is patrician – expensive, residential villas with gardens – while Sarrià retains the feel of a small Catalan town and is very charming.

TIBIDABO

The first bright, clear morning or late afternoon of your visit, head for **Tibidabo** ⑫, the 542-metre (1,778ft) peak of the Collserola range, overlooking the city. The views are breathtaking. The church of **El Sagrat Cor**, floodlit at night, built in the first half of the 20th century in neo-Romanesque and neo-Gothic style, and surmounted by a monumental figure of Christ, is one of the city's landmarks.

Spectacular view from the Torre de Collserola

To reach the summit, take the FGC train from the Plaça de Catalunya to Avda Tibidabo. From here the **Tramvia Blau**, an old-fashioned blue wooden tram, runs every day during the summer (weekends only in winter), taking you up to the funicular station, past grand villas. Don't miss the nearby **CosmoCaixa** (Tue–Sun 10am–8pm), a splendid science museum with a Planetarium that projects a 3D show using the latest technology.

From Plaça del Dr Andreu the funicular lifts you through pine woods to the top, where you have a spectacular panorama of the city, the coast and the Pyrenees. Families flock to the famous, 1950s-style amusement park, the **Parc d'Atraccions** (www.tibidabo.cat; July–Aug Wed–Sun noon–11pm, Sept–Dec, Mar–June Sat–Sun noon–9pm, with exceptions). With over 25 attractions, many of the old favourites remain but there is now a new generation of rides to experience, too. In 2012 a state-of-the-art laser show was unveiled.

The **Parc de Collserola** is a huge, green swathe that makes a great escape from the city. Families come here at weekends and summer evenings to enjoy the fresh air. There are jogging and cycling tracks, nature trails, picnic spots and *merenderos*, where you barbecue your own food.

Another high spot is the **Torre de Collserola** communications tower (www.torredecollserola.com; July–Aug Wed–Sun noon–8pm, Sept–June Sat–Sun only, with exceptions), designed by Sir Norman Foster for the 1992 Barcelona Olympics. A chic transparent lift whisks you to the top for fabulous panoramic views.

EXCURSIONS

There's a great deal to detain you in Bacelona, but just beyond the city are several sites eminently worthy of day trips. These include the holy Catalan shrine of Montserrat, the relaxed and pretty town of Sitges for beaches and museums, and the cava wine country in the region of Penedès.

MONTSERRAT

Sir Norman Foster-designed Collserola tower

Montserrat ㉝ (www.montserratvisita.com), Catalonia's most important religious retreat and the shrine of Catalan nationhood, rises out of the rather featureless Llobregat plain 48km (30 miles) northwest of Barcelona. The view from its 1,241-metre (4,075ft) summit can encompass both the Pyrenees and Mallorca, and the monastery itself can be seen from afar, surrounded by the jagged ridges that give it its name – the Serrated Mountain.

The first hermitages on the mountain may have been established by those trying to escape the Moorish

Montserrat's monastery, set high in the mountains

invasion. One was enlarged as a Benedictine monastery in the 11th century and a century later it became the repository for **La Moreneta**, the Black Madonna, a small, wooden image of a brown-faced Virgin (darkened by candle smoke) holding the infant Jesus on her lap and a globe in her right hand. The figure is said to be a carving by St Luke, later hidden by St Peter. Ever since, pilgrims – from commoners to kings – have climbed the mountain to worship the Catalan patron saint. More than a million pilgrims and tourists visit the shrine each year.

The **monastery** was burned to the ground by Napoleon's soldiers in 1808, abandoned in 1835 when all convents were sequestered by the state, and rebuilt in 1874. During the Spanish Civil War, La Moreneta was secretly replaced by a copy; the original remained hidden during the dictatorship. Although Catalan culture was suppressed, monks here continued to say Mass in Catalan.

The site of the monastery is spectacular, tucked into folds of rock high above the plain. On the eve of the saint's day, 27 April, the monks hold an all-night vigil attended by huge crowds. La Moreneta looks down from a gold-and-glass case, above and to the right of the altar in the **basilica** (7.30am–8pm, access to La Moreneta 8–10.30am, noon–6.30pm), but the faithful can touch or kiss her right hand through an opening. Each day the Escolans, the oldest boys' choir in Europe, founded in the 13th century, fill the basilica with their pure voices (Mon–Fri 1pm and 6.45pm, Sun 6.45pm, no choir June–mid-Aug and 26 Dec–8 Jan). The monastery and its underground **museum** (daily 10am–5.30pm) contain many valuable works of art, including paintings by El Greco.

Montserrat is also a popular goal for cyclists and mountain climbers who ascend the spires of rock above the building. From the monastery there are walks to other hermitages and a funicular to the **Santa Cova**, the cave sacred to the legend of the Madonna. Statues and plaques line the paths. Due to its popularity, Montserrat has a number of bars, restaurants and shops around the Plaça de la Creu. For a peaceful visit, spend the night in the hotel or former monks' cells.

GETTING THERE

Montserrat can be reached in an hour by FGC train from Barcelona's Plaça d'Espanya to either Montserrat Aeri, where a cable car continues up the side of the mountain to the monastery, or the next stop, Monistrol de Montserrat, where the more comfortable Cremallera train travels up to the monastery, for the same price. If you are driving, leave Barcelona via the Diagonal and take the A2 highway in the direction of Lleida, taking the exit to Manresa for Monistrol.

Sant Sebastià beach in Sitges

SITGES

It's easy to get to the Costa Daurada beaches from Barcelona. The coast south of the city earned its name from its broad, golden sands, in contrast to the rocky coves of the Costa Brava to the north. **Sitges ❸❹**, a favourite resort of Barceloneses, is the best place for a day trip. It's a short drive on the C32 motorway, or a 40-minute train ride from Sants or Passeig de Gràcia stations, if you get a fast train – some of them stop frequently en route. There is also a scenic coastal drive that is narrow and curvy and obviously takes longer.

Happily, the pretty little town has escaped the high-rises and tawdry atmosphere of many coastal resorts, although it does get somewhat overwhelmed by crowds in summer. There are two beaches, separated by a promontory where gleaming, whitewashed houses cluster around the church of **Sant Bartolomeu i Santa Tecla**. The biggest and best beach is **Platja d'Or** (Golden Beach), backed by a palm-lined promenade and dozens of cafés and restaurants – some of them very good indeed. North of the promontory is Sant Sebastià beach, smaller and quieter and extremely pleasant.

THREE SEASIDE MUSEUMS

Besides the beaches, Sitges is known for its appealing museums. The **Museu Cau Ferrat** is in the house built by the painter Santiago Rusiñol (1861–1931), whose collection of works by El Greco, Casas, Picasso and others is on display, along with many of his own works.

Next to Cau Ferrat is the **Museu Maricel**, a splendid house overlooking the sea – the name means 'sea and sky'. It displays a small collection of Gothic sculpture and paintings, some notable murals by Josep Maria Sert (1876–1945) and the town's art collection, with paintings by the Romantics, Lumanists and Modernists.

The nearby **Museu Romàntic** (Tue–Sat 9.30am–2pm, 3.30–6.30pm, Sun 10am–3pm), on Sant Gaudenci, displays the furniture and accoutrements of a wealthy 19th-century family, as well as a large collection of antique dolls, the Lola Anglada collection.

On the outskirts of Sitges are the villas of wealthy Barceloneses, while the pretty streets between the beach and station are geared for food and fun. Sitges has one of Spain's largest gay communities, and attracts gay travellers year-round, but particularly during the riotous February carnival. Gay and nudist beaches lie a little way beyond the other beaches of the town.

Museu Maricel

Located inland from Sitges, on the road to Vilafranca, is **Sant Pere de Ribes**, which has a 10th-century castle and a delightful Romanesque church.

SANT SADURNÍ D'ANOIA (PENEDÈS)

Cava, Catalonia's sparkling wine, comes from the **Penedès**, a pretty region south of Barcelona (about 45 minutes on the train from Sants or Plaça de Catalunya stations; by road, take the AP7 in the direction of Tarragona). These days the top-selling cavas are produced by Codorníu and Freixenet. The centre of cava production is the small town of **Sant Sadurní d'Anoia** ㉟, where several wineries offer guided tours and tastings.

The most interesting of these is **Can Codorníu** (www.codorniu.com; tel: 93-891 3342 to check opening times to arrange a visit). This is Spain's largest producer of cava and has been in the business since 1872. The family-owned winery is located on a spectacular campus, with *modernista* buildings by Gaudí's contemporary, Puig i Cadafalch. Completed in 1898, it has been declared a National Artistic and Historic Monument. Visitors to the winery are taken on a theme-park-like ride through 26km (16 miles) of atmospheric underground cellars.

Vineyards in Penedès

World-famous cava producer **Freixenet** has its headquarters next to the station (www.freixenet.es; tel: 93-891 7000; Mon–Sat 10am–6pm, Sun 10am–2.30pm, with exceptions).

There are some good restaurants in and near town, which the staff at Codorníu will be happy to tell you about. Most of them specialise in seafood accompanied, of course, by cava. If you visit the area between January and March you must try another regional dish, *calçots* – baby leeks grilled and dipped in a peppery, garlicky sauce – and so popular they actually have a fiesta in their honour at this time, called the *calçotada*.

Fiesta celebrations in Vilafranca del Penedès

VILAFRANCA DEL PENEDÈS

Some 15km (8 miles) to the south of Sant Sadurní, surrounded by vineyards, is the town of **Vilafranca del Penedès** , the capital of the Alt-Penedès region and the place where the world-renowned Torres red wine is produced.

The **Vinseum: Museu de les Cultures del Vi de Catalunya** (www.vinseum.cat; Mon–Fri 10am–2pm, 4–7pm) is said to be one of the best wine museums in Europe. It is housed in the renovated Gothic **Palau Reial**, residence of the count-kings of Barcelona-Aragón, and reopened in late 2012 following a major makeover.

The local festival (29 August–2 September), when the wine flows freely and the human towers called *castells* make their appearance, is a good time to visit the town and a great way to round off your holiday.

WHAT TO DO

SHOPPING

Barcelona is firmly on the map of European shopping capitals. As a city of eminent style and taste, it is packed full of fashion boutiques from high-street brands to top designers, antique shops, state-of-the-art home interior stores and art galleries. Design is taken very seriously here. Shopping is extremely pleasant; the city has not been totally overtaken by homogenous chain stores and shiny, modern shopping malls. Catalonia still thrives on family-owned shops, and window shopping on the Rambla de Catalunya or Passeig de Gràcia is a delight. The best items include fashionable clothing, shoes and leather products, antiques, books, high-tech design, home furnishings, objets d'art and music.

WHERE TO LOOK

Passeig de Gràcia, **Rambla de Catalunya** and **Diagonal** are great for fashion, jewellery, design and art galleries. Alternative fashion shops, galleries and street markets are dotted around the **Barri Gòtic**, **El Born** and **El Raval**. Plaça de Catalunya is the jumping-off point for some of the best shopping streets: **Portal de l'Àngel**, **Pelai** and **Carrer Portaferrisa** are always swarming with shoppers. The upper section of La Rambla has some leading fashion stores, though tacky souvenir shops are rife.

DEPARTMENT STORES AND MALLS

The major department store is **El Corte Inglés** (www.elcorte ingles.es), Spain's biggest. There is the huge, original branch on Plaça de Catalunya, one in Portal de l'Àngel, and one in the Diagonal (all open 10am–10pm). Also in Plaça de Catalunya is a large complex called **El Triangle** (www.eltriangle.es), which

The extravagant Grand Teatre del Liceu opera house

Includes Hàbitat, perfume emporium Sephora and FNAC, which has the city's best selection of national and foreign music, magazines, books, DVDs and the very latest in computer wizardry. **L'Illa** (www.lilla.com), on the Diagonal (above Plaça Francesc Macià), is one of Barcelona's best upmarket shopping malls. In **Port Vell** the Maremàgnum (www.maremagnum.es) mall is teeming with shops and open 10am–10pm, including Sundays. One of the largest and best equipped malls is **Diagonal Mar** (www.diagonalmarcentre.es) by the sea near the Forum, easily reached by metro. Barcelona's newest and most spectacular mall, **Las Arenas** (www.arenasdebarcelona.co), is in Montjuïc and opened in 2011.

Stalls at the Els Encants flea market on Plaça de les Glòries

ANTIQUES AND ART GALLERIES

Some of the best spots for antiques are in the old town, along **Banys Nous**, **de la Palla**, and **Baixada Santa Eulàlia**, between the cathedral and the Plaça del Pi. An antiques market is held every Thursday in the cathedral square. There are several individual shops around the Eixample, and **Bulevar dels Antiquaris**, at Passeig de Gràcia 57, conceals a maze of dealers.

For art purchases, explore **Consell de Cent**, in the Eixample; the **Born**, a hot gallery-browsing area; and the streets around the contemporary art museum, MACBA, in **El Raval**. There are several galleries on **Petritxol**, near Plaça del Pi, and **Montcada**, clustered around the Museu Picasso. Ceramics, ranging from traditional tiles, plates and bowls with brightly coloured glazing, to more modern creations, can be found in the streets around the cathedral and along **Montcada**. A selection of good-quality ceramics and handicrafts is sold at Art Escudellers (Escudellers 23–25). BCN Original, next to the tourist information office at Plaça de Catalunya 17, has a good selection of souvenirs and gifts. Many museum shops also sell high-quality art and design items.

Shopping hours

With the exception of department stores, fashion shops and malls, most shops close 1.30–4.30pm, but all stay open until 8pm or later. Smaller shops may close on Saturday afternoon and most stores close on Sunday.

BOOKS

Spain's publishing industry is based in Barcelona, so it's easy to find a wide assortment of books, including many titles in English. Excellent glossy books on Spanish culture, art and cookery and lots of discounted titles – many in English – are found at Happy Books (Portal de l'Àngel). Come In is an English bookshop on Balmes, while La Central in Elisabets is a haven for browsers, located in a former chapel. Laie on Pau Claris is an excellent bookshop-cum-café/restaurant. It also has branches in the CCCB (Contemporary Culture Centre) and other museums throughout the city. Hibernian Books in Gràcia (Carrer Montseny) has a wide range of second-hand English books.

DESIGN

For quintessential Catalan design, Vinçon (Passeig de Gràcia 96), Barcelona's top design emporium, is full of items such as

Markets

Barcelona's biggest and best flea market is Els Encants, which pulsates with action every Monday, Wednesday, Friday and Saturday 9am–5/6pm at Plaça de les Glòries Catalanes (Glòries metro). Some of the stuff is good, some is rubbish, but it's all good fun. For stamps, coins and memorabilia, go to the Plaça Reial on Sunday morning, or to the Sant Antoni market for records and books. Plaça Sant Josep Oriol has a weekend art fair and there is an antiques fair every Thursday (in summer) in the cathedral square.

expensive lighting and funky furniture, stylish watches, kitchen utensils, stationery and classy bags – a great place to wander and get inspired. Pilma (Diagonal 403) has good stock and low-key good taste, but less innate style; the Born area is good for trendy, original items.

FASHION

Cool fashion for men and women by Toni Miró can be found at his signature store (Antoni Miró) at Consell de Cent 349. Galician designer Adolfo Domínguez sells classic fashion at Passeig de Gràcia 32 and 89, and Diagonal 570. Nearby, at Diagonal 609, Gonzalo Comella displays labels that include Miró, Armani and Ermenegildo Zegna. Loewe in Casa Lleó Morera (Passeig de Gràcia 35) is Spain's premier leather goods store. An iconic Catalan name in fashion is the dynamic Custo-Barcelona, whose flagship store can be found in the Diagonal Mar shopping mall.

FOOD

Colmado Quílez (Rambla de Catalunya 63) is a classic Catalan grocery, with packaged goods, fine wines, cheeses and imported beer in a photogenic corner shop. For roasted nuts, dried fruits, coffee and spices, go to the 150-year-old Casa Gispert (Sombrerers 23) near Santa Maria del Mar. Escribà, at La Rambla 83, is a beautiful, century-old shop selling wonderful chocolates. For a religious experience and a history lesson with your shopping, visit Caelum (de la Palla 8), which stocks a variety of products produced by Trappist monks, such as beers, honey, candles and cheese. Downstairs is a cellar/tea room where ancient foundations of 14th-century baths were uncovered and are now on public view.

The ultimate food shopping experience in Barcelona, of course, is Mercat La Boqueria (see page 28) for fish, meat, fruit, vegetables, charcuterie and olives. It's open Monday to Saturday till 8.30pm and it's not to be missed.

ENTERTAINMENT

Piles of fresh produce at La Boqueria

While Barcelona may not be quite as fanatical about late nights as Madrid, it is still a place that really comes to life when the sun goes down. It has virtually every kind of entertainment, from cool cabarets to live jazz, rock to flamenco and world music, opera, symphony concerts, dynamic theatre and dance and a thriving bar and club scene. At night, some streets, such as La Rambla, become slow-moving rivers of people just walking and talking. The main churches and monuments are illuminated, and the city takes on a new and stimulating aspect.

Harlem Jazz Club

MUSIC, BALLET AND THEATRE

A concert at the **Palau de la Música** (Carrer del Palau de la Música 4–6; tel: 902-442 882; www.palaumusica.org), the *modernista* masterpiece, is a wonderful experience, whatever the performance is. The varied programme includes chamber and symphony concerts, contemporary music and occasionally jazz.

Barcelona's famous opera house, **Gran Teatre del Liceu** (La Rambla 51–9; tel: 93-274 6411; www.liceubarcelona. com), which was gutted by fire in 1994, reopened to general acclaim in 1999. It hosts extravagant and avant-garde productions and a short ballet season. Tickets are hard to get, despite its increased seating capacity, but worth a try. **L'Auditori** (Plaça de les Arts), home of the OBC (Barcelona Symphony Orchestra), has a 2,500-seat auditorium and a smaller one for chamber concerts (for tickets tel: 93-247 9300; www.auditori.org).

The **CaixaForum** (Av. de Francesc Ferrer I Guàrdia 6; tel: 93-476 8600) is a sophisticated cultural centre that hosts musical performances as well as exhibitions and other events.

For theatre, there is the **Teatre Nacional de Catalunya** (Plaça de les Arts; tel: 93-306 5700; www.tnc.cat), with a wide and varied programme, and the **Teatre Lliure** (Passeig de Santa Madrona; tel: 93-289 2770; www.teatrelliure.com) for good contemporary productions. Most productions are in Catalan, occasionally Spanish, and foreign companies visit at festival time. The **Mercat de les Flors** (Lleida 59; tel: 93-256 2600; www.mercatflors.org) specialises in dance and movement.

Tickets for cultural events can be booked at the information centre in Palau Virreina on La Rambla (Mon–Sat 10am–8.30pm) and at the venue's box office or online at www.telentrada.com.

FLAMENCO AND JAZZ

Flamenco is not a Catalan tradition, but some *tablaos* – live flamenco performances – are staged for tourists. Tablao Flamenco Cordobés (Las Ramblas 35; tel: 93-317 5711; www.tablaocordobes.com) is the most popular, while El Patio Andaluz (Aribau 242; tel: 93-209 3378; www.showflamencobarcelona.com) also puts on *sevillanas*, traditional Andalusian music. There are also shows twice nightly, except Monday, at El Tablao de Carmen in the Poble Espanyol on Montjuïc (Arcos 9; tel: 93-325 6895; www.tablaodecarmen.com). One of the most authentic shows is at Los Tarantos in Plaça Reial (tel: 93-319 1789; www.masimas.com/tarantos).

Live jazz can be found most nights at Harlem Jazz Club in the Gothic Quarter (Comtessa de Sobradiel 8), fused with world music and flamenco. Jamboree (www.masimas.com/jamboree), in the Plaça Reial, is also good. Luz de Gas (Muntaner 246; www.luzdegas.com) presents jazz, rock and soul, and becomes a dance venue after midnight.

NIGHTLIFE

For seasoned *juerguistas* (ravers) the Barcelona nightlife is hard to beat. From sundown to sunrise there's a venue for every taste and the streets buzz as if it were midday. For early evening don't miss atmospheric cocktail bars **Boadas** (Tallers 1), famed for its mojitos, and long-established **Dry Martini** (Aribau 162), or a terrace bar in a square in the Gràcia neighbourhood, where a young, laid-back crowd gather.

The scene really hots up after midnight, much of it centred on the Old Town, where a few remnants of the old Barri Xino mingle with hip new nightspots and restaurants like **Rita Rouge** (Plaça de la Gardunya) that turn into clubs at midnight. The Born area is still cool for classics like **Gimlet** (Santaló 46) or **Berimbau** (Passeig del Born 17), while the Plaça Reial in the Gothic Quarter has every kind of nightspot from disco **Karma** to **Sidecar** with its live gigs. Uptown, some of the original 1980s designer bars and clubs are still going strong, such as **Otto Zutz** (Lincoln 15) with its three dance floors, and **Ommsession**, hip hotel Omm's club (Rosselló 265). New on the scene, **Bling Bling** (Carrer de Tuset 10) is a very chic, upmarket club challenging these old favourites, and **Sala Apolo** (Nou de la Rambla 113) and **Razzmatazz** (Pamplona 88) are two of the coolest spots in town. Halfway up Tibidabo is **Mirablau** (Plaça del Dr Andreu 2), a bar-club with a panoramic view of the city. Irresistible

Papier-mâché gegants (giants) at a fiesta

in the summer are the beach bars or *chiringuitos* on every beach from Barceloneta to Diagonal Mar, where you can dance in the sand till dawn.

FESTIVALS

There are numerous music festivals: the **Festival de Guitarra de Barcelona** (www.theproject.es) in March–May, the **Festival Internacional de Jazz**

Listings magazines

Weekly cultural guide *Guía del Ocio* (available at newsstands or online at www.guiadelociobcn.com in Spanish) has up-to-date entertainment information, while the *Metropolitan*, a free monthly English magazine, has listings, reviews and articles (www.barcelona-metropolitan.com).

(www.theproject.es) in October and November, and the **Grec Summer Festival** of dance, music and theatre (www.bcn.cat) in July, when the cultural calendar is brimming with events ranging from avant-garde theatre to jazz concerts. Events are held all over the city, but the most impressive are at the **Grec Theatre**, an open air amphitheatre on Montjuïc (check programme and buy tickets at the Virreina Palace, La Rambla 99; see page 27).

If you're in the city during a festival you'll see the different neighbourhoods erupt into life. Food, fireworks, music and the huge papier-mâché effigies called *gegants* (giants) and their companions, the *cap grossos* (bigheads), are essential features. The *gegants* are about 4 metres (13ft) high and elaborately dressed as kings and queens, knights and ladies. *Cap grossos* are cartoon heads of well-known personalities, often accompanied by *dracs* (dragons) and *dimonis* (devils).

A constant of Catalan festivals are the *castellers*, acrobatic troupes of men, boys and girls who form human towers up to nine men high. This takes place most spectacularly at the **Festival of La Mercè**, the city's patron saint, on 24 September, in the Plaça de Sant Jaume. The **pre-Lent Carnaval** is another good excuse to dress up and hold processions and parties. Like most festivals it is accompanied by late-night bands and plenty of fireworks (see page 96 for major events).

SPORTS

The 1992 Olympics cemented Barcelona's reputation as a sports-mad city. Barceloneses are wild about Barça, their championship football (soccer) club, and are avid spectators of basketball, tennis, golf and motorsport. But they're also active sports enthusiasts, eager to escape the city for cycling, sailing or skiing, the latter only a couple of hours away in the Pyrenees.

SPECTATOR SPORTS

Barça fans at the Camp Nou stadium

The great spectator sport in Barcelona is football, and a match involving Barça (www.fcbarcelona.com), one of Europe's perennial champions, can bring the city to a standstill. The club's **Camp Nou** stadium, in the Les Corts area near the Diagonal, is the largest in Europe. Camp Nou has one of the most visited museums in Spain (Mon–Sat 10am–6.30pm, Sun 10am–2.30pm, with exceptions). Match tickets can be purchased ahead online at the club's website or on the day at the ticket office on Travessera de les Corts, but tickets can be scarce for big matches. The city does have another football club, Espanyol, who are based at the **RCDE stadium** in the suburb of Cornella de Llobregat; match tickets for their games are easier to get hold of (www.rcdespanyol.com).

The city's second favourite spectator sport is basketball. FC Barcelona Regal (www.fcbarcelona.com) play at the **Palau Blaugrana**, on the same site as Camp Nou. They share the facilities with the roller hockey, *futsal* (indoor football) and handball teams. The season runs from September to May and tickets can be purchased directly at Palau Blaugrana or online.

Tennis is also popular, and the prestigious **Real Club de Tennis Barcelona-1899** (www.rctb1899.es) off Av. Diagonal near Pedralbes, with a centre court seating 7,200, stages the Barcelona Open APT World Tour tournament each April. Spaniards have won on many occasions, with Rafael Nadal lifting the trophy seven times.

PARTICIPANT SPORTS

Recreational cycling and jogging on Montjuïc and Tibidabo is very popular, and of course swimming – whether at the city beaches or along the Costa Daurada and Costa Brava – is a prime activity. Visitors can hire skates or bikes, play golf at one of the fine courses near the city, or visit Tibidabo's **Can Caralleu sports centre** (tel: 93-204 6905; www.cemcancaralleu.cat), which has tennis, *pelota*, volleyball and two swimming pools.

Cycling is popular and tourist offices can provide a map showing recommended routes and bike lanes and advice about taking bikes on public transport. Or contact **Amics de la Bici** (Demóstenes 19; tel: 93-339 4060; www.amicsdelabici. org). On Tibidabo, the **Carretera de las Aiguas**, a path that winds along the mountain with spectacular views of the city below, is a great place to walk, jog or cycle. **Barcelona by Bike** offers easygoing tours around the city (tel: 93-268 8107; www. barcelonabybike). Bikes can be rented from **Biciclot** (Passeig

Marítim de la Barceloneta 33; tel: 93-221 9778; www.biciclot. net), where there is easy access to the Parc de la Ciutadella and the waterfront (tandems and child seats available). Alternatively, rent rollerblades from **Inercia** (Carrer Roger de Flor 10; tel. 93-486 9256; www.inercia-shop.com).

At the **Reial Club de Golf El Prat** (El Prat de Llobregat; tel: 93-728 0210), near the airport, 27 holes provide three different circuits. Clubs and carts can be hired, and there's a pool for non-participants. Other courses located nearby include **Club de Golf Sant Cugat** (Sant Cugat del Vallès; tel: 93-674 3908), just west of the city, which hires out clubs and trolleys and has a pool; and the **Terramar course** at Sitges (tel: 93-894 0580; http://golfterramar. com). For additional information, visit www.catgolf.com.

For sailing information, you can contact the **Reial Club Marítim** (tel: 93-221 4859). For water sports and equipment hire in general, try **Base Nautica de la Mar Bella** on Platja Mar Bella, Av. Litoral (tel. 93-221 0432).

Skiing in the Pyrenees is popular. Most resorts are within two hours of Barcelona; some are accessible by train, and there are cheap weekend excursions available. Information can be obtained from the **Asociació Catalana d'Estacions d'Esquí** (tel: 93-416 0194; www.lamolina.com).

CHILDREN

Barcelona is an excellent city for children. Taking young children to restaurants is a regular occurrence, so they are completely accepted. The clean beaches will keep most children and parents happy in between sightseeing, and the Port Vell waterfront has **L'Aquàrium** (Moll d'Espanya; tel: 93-221 7474; www.aquariumbcn.com), one of the largest aquariums in Europe with fascinating marine life on display. There is also a **3D Imax** film theatre in the port (tel: 93-225 1111; www.imax portvell.com). The **Zoo** (Ciutadella Park; www.zoobarcelona.

Inhabitant of the Parc Zoológic

cat), is not the best, but it's in a pleasant setting, while the park itself, with boats for hire, is fun and shady. The **Poble Espanyol** (Montjuïc), a recreation of a Spanish village, is popular with families, both locals and visitors, and manages to interest teenagers as well as children (see page 71).

Tibidabo amusement park (Parc d'Atraccions; tel: 93-211 7942; www.tibidabo.cat) is good, family fun, and kids love to arrive there on the Tramvia Blau (see page 74). As for museums, the science museum **CosmoCaixa** below the park is full of hands-on, child-friendly exhibits, including an area dedicated to three- to six-year-olds (see page 74). The **Museu de la Xocolata** (Chocolate Museum; Antic Convent de Sant Agustí, La Ribera; www.museu xocolata.cat) has tempting chocolate sculptures, while the **Museu de Cera** (Wax Museum; www.museocerabcn.com) off La Rambla at Passatge de la Banca 7, with its lifelike models, is usually a hit as well. Teenagers can spend hours watching skateboarders in front of the MACBA (Plaça dels Angels) or joining in themselves.

CALENDAR OF EVENTS

6 January Reis Mags (Three Kings' Day). Gift giving and procession.

February (second week) Feast of Santa Eulàlia, a winter *Festa Major* that's a low-key version of La Mercè (see 24 September).

February–March Carnival, preceding Lent, is a wild celebration. Sitges carnival is the best in the region.

Setmana Santa/Easter Palm Sunday processions and services on Holy Thursday/Good Friday.

23 April Feast of Sant Jordi (St George). Book and rose stalls are set up in La Rambla and Passeig de Gràcia.

27 April Feast of Virgin of Montserrat. Liturgical rituals, choir singing and *sardana* dancing.

11 May Sant Ponç. Herb fair in Carrer de l'Hospital.

Mid-June Corpus Christi. Carpets of flowers and processions in Sitges. In Barcelona 'dancing eggs' are balanced on the spray of the cathedral fountain and fountains in other courtyards in the Barri Gòtic.

23–24 June Sant Joan (St John). A major event in Catalonia, with fireworks, feasting and flowing cava.

July Grec Summer Festival of theatre, dance, classical, pop and rock music.

15–21 August Festa Major de Gràcia. Street parties, parades, fireworks and concerts in Gràcia neighbourhood.

11 September Diada. Catalan national day, with demonstrations and flag waving.

24 September La Mercè. Barcelona's week-long festival, in honour of its patron, Mare del Déu de la Mercè (Our Lady of Mercy). Fireworks, music and dancing in the streets. Head to Plaça St Jaume to see *castells*; the Ball de Gegants is a parade of huge papier-mâché figures; Correfoc is a rowdy nocturnal parade of devils and fire-spitting dragons, not to be missed.

1–23 December Santa Llúcia Fair selling Nativity figurines, art, crafts and Christmas trees in front of the cathedral.

26 December Sant Esteve (St Stephen's Day). Families meet for an even larger meal than that eaten on Christmas Day.

EATING OUT

Catalans adore eating, and especially love dining out, the epitome of social activity. They enjoy one of the finest, most imaginative cuisines in Spain, and Barcelona is the best place to sample its rich variety. The cooking is an attractive mix of haute cuisine and the traditional rustic cooking that has fed Catalans for centuries.

Barcelona's restaurants begin with a major advantage: superb ingredients, as anyone who's entered a great covered market in the city can attest. Catalan cooking is based on *cuina del mercat* – market cuisine. Fresh fish and shellfish lead the menus (even though they're often flown in from the north coast and Galicia), and fruits and vegetables are at their freshest. Mountain-cured hams and spicy sausages, spit-roasted meats and fowl with aromatic herbs are specialities. Expect *all i oli* (garlic and olive oil mayonnaise), produce from the countryside, and wild mushrooms – *bolets* – an object of obsession for people from all over Catalonia.

Barcelona's cosmopolitan population enjoys food from every Spanish region; Basque cookery is especially appreciated and Basque tapas bars have sprouted like the much-loved wild mushrooms. International cuisine used to mean French, but the number of restaurants from all over the world has exploded. Most top restaurants are in the Old Town and the Eixample, though the most lively areas are along the waterfront, in the new port and in El Born. The most exclusive restaurants tend to be in the *Barrios Altos*, uptown residential neighbourhoods. Eating out in Barcelona

Freshly prepared tapas

is a treat and can be one of the highlights of your trip. Restaurants are not cheap, but they compare favourably with those in many European and North American capitals. Sometimes menus are offered only in Catalan, so always ask if there is one in English or Castilian Spanish.

MEAL TIMES AND MENUS

Barceloneses, like all Spaniards, eat late. Lunch usually isn't eaten until 2 or 3pm. Dinner is served from about 9pm until 11.30pm, although

Dining out is a family affair

at weekends people sometimes don't sit down to dinner until midnight. You can usually get a meal at almost any time of the day, but if you enter a restaurant soon after the doors have swung open, you are likely to find yourself dining alone, or with other foreign visitors. You could always adopt the Spanish system, which is to pace yourself for the late hours by eating tapas.

Barceloneses tend to eat a three-course meal at lunchtime, including dessert and coffee. Nearly all restaurants offer a lunchtime *menú del día* or *menú de la casa*, a daily set menu that is a really good bargain. For a fixed price you'll get three courses: a starter, often soup or salad, a main dish, and dessert (ice-cream, a piece of fruit or the ubiquitous *flan*, a kind of caramel custard), plus wine, beer or bottled water, and bread. Typically, the cost is about half what you'd expect to pay if you ordered from the regular menu. The idea is for people to be able to eat economically near their workplace, though many travel home in the two-hour lunch break. It's not uncommon to share a first course, or to order *un sólo plato* – just a main course.

You can also eat cheaply in *cafeterías*, where you will usually be offered a *plat combinat* (*plato combinado* in Castilian Spanish), usually meat or fish with chips and salad, served on the same plate. Not the best way to eat, but fast and inexpensive.

Reservations are recommended at Barcelona's more popular restaurants, especially from Thursday to Saturday. Many are closed on Sunday night. Prices generally include service, but it's customary to leave a small tip, usually under 10 percent.

Your choices are not limited to restaurants and *cafeterías*. Most bars (also called *tabernas*, *bodegas* and *cervecerías*) serve food, often of a surprisingly high standard. Here you can have a selection of tapas, sandwiches (*bocadillos* in Spanish, *bocats* or *entrepans* in Catalan) or limited *plats combinats* at almost any time of the day.

Breakfast is a trivial affair in most of Spain, Barcelona included, except at hotels that offer mega-buffets as money-makers or enticements. (Check to see if breakfast is included in the room price at your hotel; if not, it's probably better to

TAPAS

Tapas – the snacks for which Spanish bars and cafés are world-famous – come in dozens of delicious varieties, from appetisers such as olives and salted almonds, to vegetable salads, fried squid, garlicky shrimps, lobster mayonnaise, meatballs, spiced potatoes, wedges of omelette, sliced sausage and cheese. The list is virtually endless, and can be surprisingly creative, especially at the now extremely popular Basque tapas joints.

A dish larger than a tapa is called a *porción*. A large serving, meant to be shared, is a *ración*, and half of this, a *media ración*. Best of all, tapas are usually available throughout the day, and are a great way to try new flavours.

try the nearest café or cafetería.) Local people usually have a coffee accompanied by bread, toast, a pastry or croissant. The occasional bar and *cafetería* may serve an 'English breakfast' of bacon and eggs.

LOCAL SPECIALITIES

The foundation of rustic Catalan cuisine is *pa amb tomàquet* – slices of rustic bread rubbed with garlic and halves of beautiful fresh tomatoes, doused with olive oil, and sprinkled with coarse salt. Another typical Catalan dish is *espinacs a la catalana*, spinach prepared with pine nuts, raisins and garlic. Others include *escudella* (a thick tasty Catalan soup); *suquet de peix* (fish and shellfish soup); *fuet* (long, salami-type sausage); and *fideus* (long, thin noodles served with pork, sausage and red pepper). A popular local fish served in a variety of ways is *rape* (angler fish), especially tasty prepared *a l'all cremat* (with roasted garlic). Other good bets are *llobina al forn* (baked sea bass) and *llenguado a la planxa* (grilled sole). You might be fooled by the Catalan word for a Spanish *tortilla* (omelette), which is *truita*, but translates as both omelette and trout. *Bacallà*, the lowly salt cod, is now served in the most distinguished restaurants in various guises and is not cheap. A *sarsuela* is a stew of fish cooked in its own juices; a *graellada de peix* is a mixed grill of fish.

Other specialities are *llebre estofada amb xocolata* (stewed hare in a bitter-sweet chocolate sauce). Barcelona's all-purpose sausage is the hearty *botifarra*, often served (in spring) with *faves a la catalana* (young broad beans stewed with bacon, onion and garlic in an earthenware casserole). *Xató* (pronounced *sha-toe*) is the endive and olive salad of Sitges, fortified with tuna or cod, and has an especially good sauce made of red pepper, anchovies, garlic and ground almonds. The word for salad of any kind is *amanida*.

Although it originates in rice-growing Valencia, the classic seafood paella is high on many visitors' lists of dishes to sample in Barcelona. Try the restaurants in Barceloneta for a paella of fresh mussels, clams, shrimp and several kinds of fish. It will take about 20 minutes to prepare. Avoid the ready-made paellas flouted by tourist-trap restaurants, especially on La Rambla.

When it comes to dessert, *flan* is ubiquitous, but there's a home-made version, the more liquid *crema catalana* (egg custard with caramelised sugar on top). If they say it's *casera* (home-made) then don't hesitate. *Mel i mato* is a treat made with honey and creamy cheese. The best sweet things are the delightful delicacies sold in pastry shops.

DRINKS

Wine is a constant at the Catalan table. In addition to an assortment of fine wines from across Spain, Barcelona presents an

El Raval's Rita Rouge, where a Venezuelan chef adds a twist to local produce

Dry Martini cocktail bar

opportunity to try some excellent regional wines. Penedès, the grape-growing region just outside Barcelona, produces some excellent wines, including cava, Spain's sparkling wine. Cava goes well with seafood and most tapas. Among Penedès reds, try Torres Gran Coronas, Raimat and Jean León. Wines from the Priorat area are superb, robust, expensive reds that rival the best in Spain. Don't be surprised to be offered red wine chilled in hot weather. White wines from the La Rueda region are generally good.

Sangría is a favourite, made of wine and fruit fortified with brandy, but it's drunk more by visitors than locals. Spanish beers, available in bottles and on draft, are generally light and refreshing. A glass of draught beer is a caña.

You'll find every kind of sherry (jerez) here. The pale, dry fino is sometimes drunk not only as an apéritif but also with soup and fish courses. Rich dark oloroso goes well after dinner. Spanish brandy varies from excellent to rough: you usually get what you pay for. Other spirits are made under licence in Spain, and are usually pretty cheap. Imported Scotch whisky is fashionable, but expensive. It is advisable to request a particular brand when asking for spirits.

Coffee is served black (solo/sol), with a spot of milk (cortado/tallat), or half and half with hot milk (con leche/amb llet). Horchata de chufa, made with ground tiger nuts, is popular in summer, and is sold in bars called horchaterías which also sell ice cream.

TO HELP YOU ORDER

Could we have a table, please? **¿Nos puede dar una mesa, por favor?**

Do you have a set menu? **¿Tiene un menú del día?**

I'd like a/an/some... **Quisiera...**

The bill, please **La cuenta, por favor**

MENU READER

a la plancha grilled
agua water
al ajillo in garlic
arroz rice
asado roasted
atún tuna
azúcar sugar
bacalao dried salt cod
bocadillo sandwich
calamares squid
cangrejo crab
caracoles snails
la carne de cerdo pork
la carne de vaca beef
cerveza beer
champiñones mushrooms
chorizo spicy sausage
chuletón T-bone steak
cordero lamb
croquetas croquettes
ensalada salad
filete steak
flan caramel custard
gambas prawns
gazpacho cold tomato soup

helado ice cream
huevo egg
jamón serrano cured ham
judías beans
langosta lobster
leche milk
lomo pork loin
marisco shellfish
mejillones mussels
morcilla black pudding
pan bread
patata potato
patatas fritas chips
pescado fish
picante spicy
pollo chicken
pulpo octopus
queso cheese
salchicha sausage
salsa sauce
ternera veal
tortilla omelette
trucha trout
verduras vegetables
vino wine

PLACES TO EAT

We have used the following symbols to give an idea of the price for an à la carte, three-course meal for one, with house wine:

€€€€ over 60 euros   **€€** 25–40 euros
€€€ 40 60 euros   **€** below 25 euros

CIUTAT VELLA (OLD TOWN)

Agut €€ *Carrer Gignàs 16, tel: 93-315 1709,* www.restaurantagut. com. Tue–Sun lunch and dinner. This small restaurant, founded in 1924, is hidden away on a small street in the Barri Gòtic behind Passeig de Colom, not far from the main post office. Relaxed and homely, it has plenty of Catalan flavour and lots of daily specials, which might include home-made cannelloni, fish or game. The excellent and huge rice dishes are meant to be shared.

Biocenter € *Carrer del Pintor Fortuny 25, tel: 93-301 4583,* www. restaurantebiocenter.es. Mon Sat lunch and dinner, Sun lunch only. Vegetarian restaurant serving huge portions in a friendly atmosphere. Located just off La Rambla, north of the Mercat La Boqueria.

Cal Pep €€–€€€ *Plaça de les Olles 8, tel: 93-310 7961,* www.calpep. com. Mon dinner only, Tue–Fri lunch and dinner, Sat lunch only. A boisterous bar in a pretty square in El Born, just off Pla del Palau, this is the place for some of the best seafood in Barcelona – if you can get a seat. Reservations are only available for groups of four or more, and there's just one row of chairs at the counter and a few tables in the back room. The counter is the place to be. The display of baby squid, octopus, fried fish and mussels is amazing. Be prepared to queue, it's worth the wait.

Can Culleretes €–€€ *Carrer d'en Quintana 5, tel: 93-317 3022,* www.culleretes.com. Tue–Sat lunch and dinner, Sun lunch only. Barcelona's oldest restaurant has served traditional Catalan food since 1786. It is cosy and informal, and serves classics like *espinacs à la catalana* (spinach with pine nuts and raisins) and *botifarra* (spicy country sausage). Fixed-price menus available weekdays. Near La Rambla but feels like a different world.

Los Caracoles €€–€€€ *Carrer d'Escudellers 14, tel: 93-301 2041*, www.loscaracoles.es. Daily lunch and dinner. 'The Snails' is famous for its chicken roasting on a spit outside, on one of the Old Quarter's busiest pedestrian streets, just south of Plaça Reial. It has been around since 1835, and while it's touristy it is fun, and you can get a fine meal of fish, game, roasted chicken or lamb, in addition, of course, to snails.

Casa Leopoldo €€€ *Carrer de Sant Rafael 24, tel: 93-441 3014*, www.casaleopoldo.com. Tue–Sat lunch and dinner, Sun lunch only. Just off the Rambla del Raval, this family-run restaurant serves excellent Catalan stews and is popular with those in the know.

La Dolça Herminia €€ *Carrer de les Magdalenes 27, tel: 93-317 0676*, www.grupandilana.com. Lunch and dinner daily. Close to Via Laietana, this smart but very reasonably priced establishment has an imaginative menu. No reservations.

Fonda España €€€ *Carrer de Sant Pau 9, tel: 93-550 0010*, www. hotelespanya.com. Mon–Sat lunch and dinner, Sun lunch only. A smart restaurant in the Hotel España, the gorgeous dining room was decorated by *modernista* architect Domènech i Montaner, while the back room has murals by Ramón Casas, a contemporary of Picasso. Renowned Michelin-starred chef, Martin Berasategui, brings new culinary delights at affordable prices. Next to the Teatre del Liceu.

El Gran Café €€–€€€ *Carrer d'Avinyó 9, tel: 93-318 7986*. Lunch and dinner daily. Looks like an English pub on the outside, but has a handsome *modernista* interior, and is well-known for its Catalan cuisine. The set menu is very good value, otherwise it is rather expensive.

Organic € *Junta de Commerç 11, tel: 93-301 0902*. Lunch and dinner daily. Serves creative organic food in a large attractive informal space not far from La Rambla. The salad and soup buffet is good when the weather is hot or cool.

Els Quatre Gats (4 Gats) €€ *Carrer de Montsió 3, tel: 93-302 4140,* www.4gats.com. Lunch and dinner daily. 'The Four Cats', which was once the hangout of Picasso and friends, serves simple Catalan fare in fabulous *modernista* surroundings. The *menú del día* (lunch only) is a good deal, but really the atmosphere's the thing.

El Quim de la Boqueria €–€€ *Mercat La Boqueria, La Rambla, tel:* *93-301 9810,* www.elquimdelaboqueria.com. Tue–Sat breakfast and lunch. This is one of several stalls in the city's biggest food market on La Rambla, where it's a treat to pull up a stool and see the freshest produce grilled before your eyes. Don't be surprised to see locals eating a hearty breakfast of pigs' trotters washed down with a glass of red wine.

Rodrigo € *Carrer de l'Argenteria 67, tel: 93-310 3020.* Wed–Mon lunch and dinner, Tue lunch only. A real family-run local bar, not far from the church of Santa Maria del Mar, serving delicious set menus at a good price. Don't miss their *vermut* house specialty.

Senyor Parellada €€–€€€ *Carrer de l'Argenteria 37, tel: 93-310* *5094,* www.senyorparellada.com. Lunch and dinner daily. An attractive, popular restaurant in La Ribera, close to the church of Santa Maria del Mar. Both the surroundings and the creative Catalan menu are sophisticated but unpretentious.

Sesamo € *Carrer de Sant Antoni Abat 52, tel: 93-441 6411.* Tue–Sun breakfast, lunch and dinner. A bit off the beaten track, close to Sant Antoni market on the western edge of El Raval, this inviting vegetarian restaurant is well worth a visit with its fantastic range of dishes and an excellent tapas tasting menu.

Shunka €€–€€€ *Carrer del Sagristans 5, tel: 93-412 4991.* Lunch and dinner Tue–Sun. Try sushi, sashimi and much more at this excellent Japanese restaurant hidden behind the cathedral. It's all cooked before your eyes.

TAPAS BARS

Bar Pinotxo €–€€ *Mercat La Boqueria, La Rambla, tel: 93-317 1731.* Breakfast and lunch daily. This tiny, plain-looking bar with a handful of stools is surrounded by La Boqueria's mesmerising produce. It's a terrific place to stop if you are shopping or sightseeing and your stomach's beginning to growl. The fish, as you would imagine, is incredibly fresh. Full lunch menu also available (recited orally, so it helps to know what some of the items are).

Euskal Etxea €€ *Placeta de Montcada 1–3, tel: 93-343 5410*, www. euskaletxeataberna.com. Lunch and dinner daily. A great Basque tapas bar with a huge choice that has quickly established itself as a firm local favourite. Excellent meals served in the restaurant area, which are more expensive. At the bottom of Carrer de Montcada, south of the Museu Picasso.

Irati €–€€ *Carrer del Cardenal Casañas 17, tel: 93-302 3084*, www. iratitavernabasca.com. Lunch and dinner daily. In the same group as Euskal Etxea (see above) this immensely popular Basque tapas joint, just off La Rambla at the edge of the Barri Gòtic, is always packed. At lunchtime and in early evening, heaving trays of tapas (*pintxos* in Basque) are laid out on the bar. It's a bit like a party, except that you have to keep track of the number of tapas and the glasses of wine or beer you've had, and the cheerful attendants tally it all up before you leave. Full menu available too.

La Vinya del Senyor € *Plaça Santa Maria 5, tel: 93-310 3379.* Lunch and dinner daily. Delightful wine bar with a large terrace overlooking the facade of Santa Maria del Mar, in the Born. Offers interesting wines and *cava* by the glass, and a few select tapas to absorb the alcohol.

El Xampanyet € *Carrer de Montcada 22, tel: 93-319 7003.* Tue–Sun lunch and dinner. Situated near the Museu Picasso and El Born, this tiled bar specialises in cava (hence the name, which is Catalan for champagne) and some of the best tinned tapas in town, especially the anchovies. A classic.

EIXAMPLE

La Bodegueta € *Rambla de Catalunya 100, tel: 93-215 4894*. Daily breakfast, lunch and dinner. It's easy to pass by this simple *bodega*, on the corner of La Rambla and Carrer de Provença, without even noticing it. Regulars pop in at any hour for *jamón serrano* (smoked ham) and a glass of Rioja. Good wine selection. No credit cards.

La Botiga € *Rambla de Catalunya 27, tel: 93-306 9668*, www.la botigarestaurant.com. Lunch and dinner daily. Great value, healthy Catalan dishes served with a modern twist in original, up-to-the-minute surroundings. One of three Botiga restaurants in the Eixample area; this one is within walking distance of Passeig metro station. It stays open until midnight.

Casa Calvet €€€–€€€€ *Carrer de Casp 48, tel: 93-412 4012*, www.casacalvet.es. Mon–Sat lunch and dinner. Located on the ground floor of one of Antoni Gaudí's first apartment buildings, Casa Calvet exudes an elegant *modernista* ambience. The service is extraordinary, and the tables are spaced well apart; some even occupy private booth areas. The Catalan menu is excellent and fairly priced. Nearest metro is Urquinaona.

Cinc Sentits €€€€ *Carrer d'Aribau 58, tel: 93-323 9490*, www.cinc sentits.com. Tue–Sat lunch and dinner. An ideal choice for foodies: Michelin-starred chef Jordi Artal's tasting menu is a guaranteed gourmet experience and a good example of new Catalan cuisine. It's at the intersection of the streets d'Aribau and d'Aragó.

Jaume de Provença €€€–€€€€ *Carrer de Provença 88, tel: 93-430 0029*. Tue–Sat lunch and dinner, Sun lunch only. Even after nearly 30 years this restaurant is still considered to be a pioneer of creative cuisine in Barcelona and is correspondingly popular. Nearest metro is Entença.

Madrid-Barcelona €€ *Carrer d'Aragó 284, tel: 93-215 7027*. Lunch and dinner daily. Located just off Passeig de Gràcia, this pleasantly old-fashioned place has a good selection of Catalan and regional Spanish dishes.

Moments €€€€ *Hotel Mandarin Oriental, Passeig de Gràcia 38–48, tel: 93-151 8781*, www.mandarinoriental.com. Tue–Sat lunch and dinner. With a Michelin star, Moments is certainly impressive and proving a popular chic, fine-dining venue. Overseen by the only female chef to hold seven Michelin stars, Carme Ruscalleda, the menu sees a return to traditional Catalan roots. Expensive, but for that special treat it takes some beating.

Taktika Berri €€–€€€ *Carrer de València 169, tel: 93-453 4759.* Mon–Fri lunch and dinner, Sat lunch only. Basque cooking is the finest regional cuisine in Spain, and Basque restaurants are popping up everywhere. One of the best in Barcelona is this family-owned and operated tapas bar and restaurant in a converted textile workshop, close to the intersection of streets València and Muntaner. The *pintxos* (tapas) are excellent, as are their creative entrées. Try the splendid desserts.

Tapas 24 €–€€ *Carrer de la Diputació 269, tel: 93-488 0977.* Daily lunch and dinner. At this trendy bar, not far from Girona metro, you can taste classic tapas by maestro Carles Abellan, one of the new generation of Catalan star chefs. You might have to queue, but it's worth it and the bustling atmosphere is absorbing. Sit at the bar or a pavement table.

Tragaluz €€€–€€€€ *Passatge de la Concepció 5, tel: 93-487 0621*, www.grupotragaluz.com. Lunch and dinner daily. Barcelona's love affair with food comes to life in this trendy, colourful restaurant on a tiny passageway off Passeig de Gràcia. After a complete overhaul in 2011 Tragaluz (Skylight), where you can dine under a glass roof, has been rejuvenated with a new fresh approach. The Mediterranean cuisine still hits the mark but with a lighter touch. Alternatively you can dine on oysters, sushi or Japanese grilled food at the bars downstairs.

WATERFRONT/PORT OLÍMPIC

Agua €€–€€€ *Passeig Marítim 30, tel: 93-225 1272*, www.gru potragaluz.com. Lunch and dinner daily. Almost on the beach, with indoor and outdoor tables, the modern and attractive Agua gets very busy, so booking is essential, especially if you want to sit on the terrace. Well-prepared fish, rice dishes such as risottos, and imaginative vegetarian dishes.

Can Ganassa €–€€ *Plaça de la Barceloneta 6, tel: 93-221 7586.* Lunch and dinner daily. A popular seafood restaurant on the main square in Barceloneta serving excellent fish dishes as well as a wide array of delicious tapas and sandwiches.

Can Majó €€–€€€ *Carrer de l'Almirante Aixada 23, tel: 93-221 5455,* www.canmajo.es. Tue–Sat lunch and dinner, Sun lunch only. It's difficult to find a really authentic paella, but at this Barceloneta classic you can't go wrong. Pleasant dining rooms and a terrace facing the sea.

L'Elx al Moll €€–€€€ *Maremàgnum, Moll d'Espanya, local 9, tel: 93-225 8117,* www.elxrestaurant.es. Lunch and dinner daily. A dependable seafood restaurant famed for its rice dishes from Valencia. Its terrace, hidden behind the shopping centre and overlooking the fishing boats in the port, is in one of the best positions you could wish for – almost like being at sea.

Restaurant 7 Portes €€€ *Passeig d'Isabel II 14, tel: 93-319 3033,* www.7portes.com. Lunch and dinner daily. Not far from the *Cap de Barcelona* artwork, this is one of Barcelona's most venerable institutions, now sympathetically restored, and a favourite for business meals and special occasions since 1836. Restaurant 7 Portes (meaning seven doors) is famous for its rice dishes; favourites include black rice with squid in its own ink and an assortment of paellas. Portions are very large, the dining rooms are elegant and the waiters are old-style attentive.

Xiringuito Escribà €€–€€€ *Avinguda Litoral Mar 42, Platja Bogatell, tel: 93-221 0729.* Daily lunch and dinner. Lots of imaginative fish and rice dishes in this down-to-earth, family-run establishment, right by the beach, east of Port Olímpic. And, yes, they are the same Escribà family that is renowned for their chocolates and pastries, so the puddings are guaranteed to be marvellous.

GRÀCIA AND ABOVE THE DIAGONAL

Bilbao €€–€€€ *Carrer del Perill 33, tel: 93-458 9624*. Mon–Sat lunch and dinner. Best at lunch time when the local crowd are there, this bustling restaurant has heaps of atmosphere and uses the freshest market produce. It's across the Avinguda Diagonal northwest of Diagonal metro, off Carrer de Corsega.

Botafumeiro €€€€ *Carrer Gran de Gràcia 81, tel: 93-218 4230*, www.botafumeiro.es. Lunch and dinner daily. This is Barcelona's top seafood restaurant and it is said to be the King of Spain's favourite. It's large and informal, with lots of action. Much of the fresh seafood is flown in daily from the owner's home territory, Galicia. You can get great shellfish and seafood tapas here (which keeps costs down). To get a seat at the seafood bar, visit off-hours, earlier than local people would eat – as the restaurant opens at 1pm for lunch, and 7–8pm for dinner. Just above the Diagonal, at the beginning of the Gràcia neighbourhood.

A–Z TRAVEL TIPS

A Summary of Practical Information

A

ACCOMMODATION (see also the list of Recommended Hotels starting on page 133)

Following fevered construction over the last decade, as well as renovation of old buildings and palaces, there are about 340 hotels in the city with still more on the way. This supply makes it possible to get some good deals off-season, especially if booked online in advance. It can still be difficult to find a central hotel when a trade fair is taking place or over main holiday periods, though there are plenty of other options. Tourist apartments are the new favourite, many old buildings having been converted into apartments for this sole purpose. A few guesthouses (hostals, pensions) and even youth hostels (albergs juvenils) are becoming 'boutique', and B&Bs are on the rise. Hotels can be booked via the tourist office (tel: 93-285 3834, www.barcelonaturisme.com).

For apartment rental, try the following agencies: Apartments Inside Barcelona (www.inside-bcn.com); Oh-Barcelona (www.oh-barcelona.com); Destination BCN (www.destinationbcn.com); Visit Barcelona (www.visit-bcn.com). For B&Bs try BCN Rooms (www.bcnrooms.com).

I'd like a double/single room. **Quisiera una habitación doble/ sencilla.**
with/without bath/shower **con/sin baño/ducha**
double bed **cama matrimonial**
What's the rate per night? **¿Cuál es el precio por noche?**
Is breakfast included? **¿Está incluido el desayuno?**

AIRPORTS

Barcelona's international airport, **El Prat de Llobregat** (tel: 902-404 704, www.aena.es) is 12km (7 miles) south of the city. You can get into Barcelona by train, bus or taxi. The national train service, RENFE (tel: 902-320 320, www.renfe.com), runs trains from the airport every half hour, stopping at Estació de Sants and Passeig de Gràcia, taking about 30 minutes. The fare is about €3.60, though it is worth buying a T10 card (see page 131). Two different Aerobuses (tel: 93-415 6020, www.aerobusbcn.com) depart every 10 minutes from each terminal for Plaça de Catalunya, daily 6.15am–1am, stopping at several points en route. The fare is €5.65 single, €9.75 return. Taxis charge about €30 to the city centre. Agree a fare before you start. They can charge extra for luggage.

B

BICYCLE RENTAL

Cycles can be rented at several outlets, such as Budget Bikes on Carrer Unió (tel: 93-304 1885, www.budgetbikes.eu), or Green Bikes on Carrer d'Ataülf 8 (tel: 93-315 1375; www.greenbikesbarcelona.com); both offer tours.

BUDGETING FOR YOUR TRIP

Barcelona has become much more expensive than it used to be and is on a par with other major European cities in many respects.

Transport to Barcelona. By budget airline or via Girona or Reus, getting to Barcelona can be the cheapest part of your trip, from as little as €30 off-season, but obviously much more (€150–300 or more) on scheduled flights or from outside Europe. Buy in advance for the best deals.

Accommodation. Most hotels do not include breakfast or the 10 percent VAT in their prices. Youth hostel €18–25 per person in a dorm; €40–60 in a *pension*; €90–225 en suite double room; €225–450 top end.

Meals. Restaurants are no longer cheap, but good deals can be found. The *menú del día*, a fixed-price midday meal, is excellent value from €12 upward. Spanish wines are usually reasonably priced, even in fine restaurants. A three-course evening meal in a mid-range restaurant with house wine: €25–50 per person.

Drinks. Mineral water €1.50–3; coffee €1.50–4; fresh orange juice €3–4; *caña* (small draught beer) €2–6; glass of wine €2–3.50; spirit with mixer €3–6 or higher in clubs.

Local transport. Public transport within the city – buses and the metro – is inexpensive (see page 130) and taxis are reasonably priced.

Attractions. Museums and attractions range from free to over €17. Most municipal museums are free from 3pm on Sundays. The Art Ticket (www. articketbcn.org) is good value at €30, as it allows entrance to seven art centres. Purchase at one of the centres or at tourist offices.

C

CAR HIRE

Unless you plan to travel a good deal throughout Catalonia, there is no need to hire a car. Barcelona has considerable parking problems and general congestion, and a car is more trouble than it's worth.

If you do wish to hire a car, however, major international and Spanish companies have offices in the airport and in the city centre. A value-added tax (IVA) of 16 percent is added to the total charge, but will have been included if you have pre-paid before arrival (lowest rates are normally found online). Shorter rentals usually cost more per day than longer ones; three days' rental for a medium-sized family car costs €250–300 (more in peak season). Fully comprehensive insurance is required and should be included in the price; confirm that this is the case. Most companies require you to pay by credit card, or use your card as a deposit/guarantee. You must be over 21 and have had a licence for at least 6 months. A national driver's licence will suffice for EU nationals; others need an international licence.

I'd like to rent a car **Quisiera alquilar un coche**
for tomorrow **para mañana**
for one day/a week **por un día/una semana**

> Please include full insurance. **Haga el favor de incluir el seguro a todo riesgo.**
> Fill it up, please. **Lleno, por favor.**
> May I return it to the airport? **¿Puedo dejarlo al aeropuerto?**

CLIMATE

Barcelona's mild Mediterranean climate assures sunshine most of the year and makes freezing temperatures rare even in the depths of winter (December to February). Spring and autumn are the most agreeable seasons for visiting. Midsummer can be hot and humid; at times a thick smog hangs over the city. Average temperatures are given below.

	J	F	M	A	M	J	J	A	S	O	N	D
°F	49	51	54	59	64	72	75	75	71	63	56	51
°C	9	10	12	14	18	22	24	24	22	18	13	11

CLOTHING

Barceloneses are very stylish and fashion-conscious. Smart-casual clothing is what visitors generally need. Men are expected to wear a jacket in better restaurants. You won't see many local people eating out in shorts and trainers, except in beachside cafés. From November to April you'll need a warm jacket or jumper and raincoat. The rest of the year, light summer clothing is in order.

CRIME AND SAFETY

You should exercise caution and be on your guard against pickpockets and bag snatchers (be wary of people offering 'assistance'), especially on or near La Rambla, the old city (particularly El Raval) and other major tourist areas, such as La Sagrada Família and crowded spots such as markets. Take the same precautions as you would at home. Photocopy personal documents and leave the originals in your hotel.

The blue-clad, mobile anti-crime squads are out in force on the Ramblas and principal thoroughfares. Should you be the victim of a crime, make a *denuncia* (report) at the nearest police station *(comisaría* – vital if you are going to make an insurance claim). The main one in the Old Town is at Nou de la Rambla 76–78, or call the Mossos d'Esquadra on 088 or 112. As from 2012 you can also report theft at most city hotels.

> I want to report a theft. **Quiero denunciar un robo.**
> My handbag/wallet/passport has been stolen. **Me han robado el bolso/la cartera/el pasaporte.**
> Help! Thief! **¡Socorro! ¡Ladrón!**

D

DISABLED TRAVELLERS

Barcelona has plenty of hotels with facilities (see www.barcelona-access.com, or check with the tourist office). Many museums and historic buildings are wheelchair-accessible. The beaches have suitable access, and there are many adapted public toilets. Some bus and metro lines have facilities for disabled travellers (see www.tmb.cat). For adapted taxi information, contact 93-420 8088.

DRIVING

In the event of a problem, drivers need a passport, a valid driving licence, registration papers and Green Card international insurance.

Road Conditions. Roads within Barcelona are very congested and the ring roads around the city can be confusing. Roads and highways outside Barcelona are excellent, though you'll have to pay a toll *(peaje/peatje)* on most motorways *(autopistas)*. To cross into France via the La Jonquera border (160km/100 miles) from Barcelona, take the AP7 or E15 motorway. For road information, tel: 900-123 505.

Rules and Regulations. Your car should display a nationality sticker. Front and rear seatbelts, a spare set of bulbs, visibility vests and two warning triangles are compulsory. Most fines for traffic offences are payable on the spot. Drive on the right, overtake on the left and give right of way to vehicles coming from the right (unless your road is marked as having priority). Speed limits are 120kmh (75mph) on motorways, 100kmh (62mph) on dual carriageways, 90kmh (56mph) on main roads, 50kmh (30mph), or as marked, in urban areas. Speed checks are regular. The roads are patrolled by the Mossos d'Esquadra. The permitted blood-alcohol level is low and penalties stiff.

¡Alto! Stop!
Aparcamiento Parking
Autopista Motorway
Ceda el paso Give way (yield)
Cruce peligroso Dangerous crossroads
Curva peligrosa Dangerous bend
Despacio Slow
Peligro Danger
Prohibido adelantar No overtaking (passing)
Prohibido aparcar No parking

Road signs. You may see the following written signs in Spanish:
Parking. Finding a place to park can be difficult in Barcelona. Look for 'blue zones' (denoted by a blue 'P'), which are metered areas, or underground parking garages (also marked with a big blue-and-white 'P'). Green zones are reserved for residents with permits.
Breakdowns and Assistance. In emergencies, tel: **112**.

Registration papers **Permiso de circulación**
Is this the right road for...? **Es ésta la carretera hacia...?**

Full tank, please. **Lléne el depósito, por favor**.
normal/super **normal/super**
Please check the oil/tyres/battery. **Por favor, controle el aceite/los neumáticos/la batería.**
Can I park here? **¿Se puede aparcar aquí?**
My car has broken down. **Mi coche se ha estropeado.**
There's been an accident. **Ha habido un accidente.**
(International) driving licence **Carnet de conducir (internacional)**
Car registration papers **Permiso de circulación**
Green card **Tarjeta verde**

E

ELECTRICITY

The standard is 220 volts. Power sockets (outlets) take round, two-pin plugs, so you will need an international adapter plug.

an adapter/a battery **un transformador/una pila/una batería**

EMBASSIES AND CONSULATES

All embassies are in Madrid, but almost all Western European countries have consulates in Barcelona:

Canada: Pl. de Catalunya 9, 1º, 2a, tel: 93-270 3614, www.canadainter national.gc.ca.

Ireland: Gran Vía Carles III 94, tel: 93-491 5021.

New Zealand: Travessera de Gràcia 64, 2º, tel: 93-209 0399.

South Africa: Parc Empresarial Mas Blau II, c/ Alta Ribargorça, 6–8, El Prat de Llobregat, tel: 93-506 9100.

UK: Avinguda Diagonal 477, 13º, tel: 93-366 6200, www.ukinspain.fco. gov.uk.

US: Passeig de la Reina Elisenda 23, tel: 93-280 2227, http://barcelona.usconsulate.gov.

EMERGENCIES (see also Police, and Crime and Safety)

General emergencies: **112**

Mossos d'Esquadra (Autonomous Catalan Police): **088**

Municipal (city) police: **092**

Fire: **080**

Ambulance: **061**

Police! **¡Policía!**
Fire! **¡Fuego!**
Stop! **¡Para!/¡Deténagase!**
Help! **¡Socorro!**
Thief! **¡Ladrón!**

GAY AND LESBIAN TRAVELLERS

Barcelona has an active gay community and scores of clubs and nightlife options. The gay and lesbian hotline is 900-601 601. The free magazine *Nois* contains information and listings (www.revistanois.com).

GETTING THERE

By Air (see also Airports). Barcelona's airport is linked by regularly scheduled, daily non-stop flights from across Europe. Some flights from the US and Canada are direct; others go through Madrid (or in some cases, Lisbon). From Australia, Singapore and New Zealand, regular one-stop flights go directly to Barcelona or Madrid. Flying times: London, about 2 hours; New York, approximately 8 hours.

Iberia, the Spanish national airline, covers most countries in shared arrangements with their own carriers. Contact Iberia in the UK: tel: 0870-609 0500, www.iberia.com.

As well as regularly scheduled flights there is a good choice of discounts and charter flights from companies such as EasyJet (www.easyjet.com). As well as flying to **El Prat**, Ryanair (www.ryanair.com) flies to **Girona** (90km/56 miles from Barcelona) and **Reus** (80km/50 miles from Barcelona) from several UK cities. Both airports have shuttle-bus connections to Barcelona (check timetables – Girona: www.sagales.com; Reus: www.igualadina.com). **Lleida-Alguaire** airport in Western Catalonia, which opened in 2010, receives some charter flights from the UK. Spanish airline Vueling (www.vueling.com) is a budget airline.

By Sea. Balearia has a service to/from Ibiza, Mallorca and Menorca (tel: 966-428 700; www.balearia.com). Acciona-Trasmediterránea (Moll Sant Bertran 3; tel: 902-454 645; www.trasmediterranea.es) also operates ferries to the Balearic islands. Grimaldi Ferries (www.grimaldi-ferries.com) go to/from Rome.

By Rail. The Spanish rail network has been greatly modernised in recent years. Nowadays you can catch high-speed, sleeper services to Barcelona from several European destinations. The Elipsos Trenhotel (www.elipsos.com) arrives at Estació de França station in Barcelona from Paris, Milan and Zurich. More high-speed links are expected with the opening of the new La Sagrera station. Trains run four times a day between Barcelona Sants station and Montpellier (www.raileurope.co.uk), where you can connect with the TGV, the French high-speed train. The AVE, the Spanish high-speed train, runs several times a day between Barcelona and Madrid.

RENFE is the Spanish national rail network (tel: 902-320 320, www.renfe.es). Local trains in Catalonia, Ferrocarrils Generalitat de Catalunya (FGC; www.fgc.cat), are serviced by the Catalan government.

RENFE honours InterRail, Rail Europe and Eurail cards (the latter sold only outside Europe), and offers substantial discounts to people under 26 and senior citizens (over 65). It is well worthwhile finding out about current discount tickets from a travel agency, station, or, in Barcelona, from the information desk in Sants station or by phoning RENFE on the number given above.

By Car. The highways outside Barcelona are generally excellent. The AP7 motorway leads to Barcelona from France and northern Catalonia; the AP2 leads to Barcelona from Madrid, Zaragoza and Bilbao. From Valencia or the Costa del Sol, take the E15 north.

By Bus. Several bus companies operate a service to Barcelona, the largest of which is Eurolines (tel: 902-405 040 or 93-367 4400, www.eurolines.es). Most arrive at the bus station Barcelona Nord (tel: 902-260 606), but some go to Estació d'Autobusos Sants. For more information and schedules, see www.barcelonanord.com.

GUIDES AND TOURS

English-speaking, licensed guides and interpreters may be arranged through the Barcelona Guide Bureau (tel: 93-268 2422; www.barcelonaguidebureau.com).

Tours by bus: Barcelona Bus Turístic (www.barcelonabusturistic.cat) offers a tour with three different routes; hop on and off as you please. Two depart from Plaça de Catalunya, one from Port Olímpic from 9am daily; all stops have full timetables. Complete journey time is about 2 hours, or 40 minutes for the Port Olímpic route. Tickets may be purchased on board or in advance at Turisme de Barcelona on Plaça de Catalunya (tel: 93-285 3832).

On foot: Barcelona Walking Tours runs English-speaking, guided tours of the Gothic quarter daily at 9.30am. Walks (lasting 2 hours) begin at Turisme de Barcelona (Plaça de Catalunya, tel. 93-285 3832). At 3pm on Tuesdays, Thursdays and Saturdays there is also a Picasso tour. Walks should be booked in advance at a tourist office. Other themed walks are available.

H

HEALTH AND MEDICAL CARE

Visitors from EU countries with corresponding health insurance facilities are entitled to medical and hospital treatment under the Spanish social security system – you need a European Health Insurance Card (EHIC), obtainable from post offices or online. However, it does not cover everything and it is advisable to take out private medical insurance, which should be part of a travel insurance package. The water is safe to drink, but bottled water is always safest.

In an emergency, go to a main hospital: Hospital Sant Pau on Carrer de Sant Antoni Maria Claret 167 (behind the Sagrada Família, tel: 93-291 9000); Hospital Clinic on Carrer de Casanova 143 (tel: 93-227 5400); Hospital Cruz Roja on Carrer Dos de Maig 301 (tel: 93-433 1551). For an ambulance, make your way to an *ambulatorio* (medical centre) or tel: **061**.

Pharmacies *(farmacias)* open during normal business hours but there is always one in each district that remains open all night and on holidays. The location and phone number of this *farmacia de guardia* is posted on the door of all the others, and carried in daily newspapers. Tel: **010** for this information.

Where's the nearest (all-night) pharmacy? **¿Donde está la farmacia (de guardia) más cercana?**
I need a doctor/dentist. **Necesito un médico/dentista.**

L

LANGUAGE

Both Catalan *(català)* and Castilian Spanish *(castellano)* are official languages in Catalonia; everyone in Barcelona who speaks Catalan can speak Castilian Spanish but many will not unless absolutely necessary. Street signs are in Catalan. Spanish (Castilian) will get you by, so most of the language tips in this section are given in Spanish.

English – *Catalan* – **Castilian**
Good morning – *Bon dia* – **Buenos días**
Good afternoon – *Bona tarda* – **Buenas tardes**
Goodnight – *Bona nit* – **Buenas noches**
Goodbye – *Adéu* – **Adiós**
Hello – *Hola* – **Hola**
See you later – *Fins desprès* – **Hasta luego**
Please – *Si us plau* – **Por favor**
Thank you – *Gràcies* – **Gracias**
You're welcome – *De res* – **De nada**
Welcome – *Benvinguts* – **Bienvenido**
Do you speak English? –¿*Parla anglés?* –¿**Habla inglés?**
I don't understand – *No ho entenc* – **No entiendo**
How much is it? –¿*Quant es?* –¿**Cuánto vale?**
Open/closed – *obert/tancat* – **abierto/cerrado**

M

MAPS

The *Guía Urbana de Barcelona* handbook is the most comprehensive and useful street map, but more manageable maps are available at the tourist office or on newsstands on La Rambla.

I'd like a street plan/a road map of this region **Quisiera un plano de la ciudad/un mapa de carreteras de esta región**

MEDIA

Most European newspapers and the Paris-based *International Herald Tribune* are sold on the day of publication at newsstands in the Ramblas and Passeig de Gràcia and in FNAC in Plaça de Catalunya. Principal European and American magazines are also widely available. *Metropolitan*, Barcelona's first monthly magazine in English, is free and has useful listings. For Spanish speakers the *Guía del Ocio (Leisure Guide)* lists bars and restaurants, along with cinema, theatre and concert performances.

MONEY

Currency *(moneda)*. The monetary unit of Spain is the euro (symbolised €). Notes are issued in denominations of 5, 10, 20, 50, 100, 200 and 500 euros. Coins in circulation are 1, 2, 5, 10, 20 and 50 cents, and 1 and 2 euros.

Currency exchange *(cambio)*. Banks and *cajas/caixes* (savings banks) are the best place to exchange currency, offering the best rates with no commission. Many travel agencies and currency exchange offices (displaying a *cambio* sign) also exchange foreign currency, and stay open outside banking hours. Be wary of those advertising 'no commission' – their rates are much lower, so you are in effect paying a hefty commission. Banks and exchange offices pay slightly more for travellers' cheques than for cash. Always take your passport when you go to change money.

Credit cards *(tarjetas de crédito)*. Photo identification is usually requested when paying with a card. Some smaller restaurants will not accept cards.

Travellers' cheques *(cheques de viajero)*. Hotels, shops, restaurants and travel agencies cash travellers' cheques, and so do some banks, where the process is more complicated, but you are likely to get a better rate. You will always need your passport.

Where's the nearest bank/currency exchange office?
¿Dónde está el banco/la casa de cambio más cercana?

I want to change some pounds/dollars **Quiero cambiar libras/dólares**

Do you accept travellers' cheques? **¿Acceptan cheques de viajero?**

Can I pay with a credit card? **¿Se puede pagar con tarjeta?**

How much is that? **¿Cuánto es/Cuánto vale?**

O

OPENING TIMES

Shops. The bigger stores and shopping malls open 10am–9.30pm, but smaller shops close in the early afternoon (for lunch). Usual hours are Mon–Sat 9am–1.30pm and 4.30–8pm or later, although these do vary.

Banks. Generally open Mon–Fri 8.30am–2pm; in winter also Sat 8.30am–1pm.

Government offices and most businesses. Open Mon–Fri 8/9am–2pm and 4–6/7pm. In summer, many businesses work *horas intensivas*, from 8am–3pm, to avoid the hottest part of the day.

Museums. Most Tue–Sat 10am–8pm and Sun 10am–2.30pm. Some close for lunch. Most close on Mondays, with exceptions. Some have later hours in summer on Thursday and Friday, often with bar service.

P

POLICE

In Barcelona, dial **092** for municipal (city) police and **088** for the autonomous Catalan police. The main police station in the Old Town is at Nou de la Rambla 76–78.

Where's the nearest police station? **¿Dónde está la comisaría más cercana?**

POST OFFICES

Post offices are identified by yellow-and-white signs with a crown and the words 'Correos y Telégrafos'. The postal system is pretty reliable. Opening hours are usually Mon–Fri 9am–2pm and Sat 9am–1pm. The central post office, in Plaça Antoni López (tel: 93-486 8302), at the port end of Via Laietana, is open Mon–Fri 8.30am–9.30pm and Sat 8.30am–2pm.

Stamps *(sellos)* can be purchased at the post office or more easily at *estancos/estancs* (tobacconists) – look for the brown-and-yellow sign that reads 'Tabacs'. Allow about one week for delivery to North America, and 4–5 days to the UK. To speed things up, send a letter *urgente* (express) or *certificado* (registered). Postboxes are yellow.

Where is the post office? **¿Dónde está el correo?**
A stamp for this letter/ postcard, please. **Por favor, un sello para esta carta/tarjeta postal**
I'd like to send this letter. **Me gustaría enviar esta carta.**
  airmail **vía aérea**
  express (special delivery) **urgente**
  registered **certificado**
How long will it take to arrive? **¿Cuánto tarda en llegar?**

PUBLIC HOLIDAYS

1 January *Año Nuevo*, New Year's Day
6 January *Epifanía/Los Reyes*, Epiphany
1 May *Fiesta de Trabajo*, Labour Day
24 June *San Juan*, St John's Day
15 August *Asunción*, Assumption
11 September *La Diada*, Catalan National Day
24 September *La Mercè (Mercedes)*, Barcelona's patron saint
1 November *Todos los Santos*, All Saints' Day
6 December *Día de la Constitución*, Constitution Day

8 December *Inmaculada Concepción*, Immaculate Conception
25–26 December *Navidad*, Christmas
Movable dates:
Feb/March *Mardi Gras*, Shrove Tuesday (Carnival)
Late March/April *Viernes Santo*, Good Friday
Late March/April *Lunes de Pascua*, Easter Monday
Mid-June *Corpus Christi*, Corpus Christi

TELEPHONES

Spain's country code is **34**. Barcelona's local area code, **93**, must be dialled before all phone numbers, even for local calls and from abroad (00 34 93 etc).

Most phone booths *(cabinas)* operate with coins and cards; international phone credit cards can also be used. For most calls at payphones, it's easier to use a phone card *(tarjeta telefónica)*, purchased at any post office or estanc (look for the sign 'Tabacos' or 'Tabacs').

To make an international call, dial **00** for an international line + the country code + phone number, omitting any initial zero. Calls are cheaper after 10pm on weekdays, after 2pm on Saturday, and all day Sunday. Dial **1009** for operator assistance within Spain, **1008** for assistance within Europe and North Africa and **1005** for the rest of the world.

You can also make calls at public telephone offices called *locutorios*. A clerk will place the call for you and you pay for it afterwards. These tend to double as internet centres too.

It can be very costly using your mobile in Spain and texting is by far the cheapest way of keeping in touch. Frequent callers might consider buying a SIM card for Spain, which can be bought in advance of your trip. The main providers in Spain are Vodafone, Orange, Moviestar and Yoigo. To phone the UK from your mobile dial 00 (+) 44 and the number, omitting the first 0.

TIME ZONES

Spanish time is the same as that in most of Western Europe – Greenwich Mean Time plus one hour. Clocks go forward one hour in spring and back one hour in autumn, so Spain is generally one hour ahead of London.

TIPPING

Since a service charge is normally included on hotel and restaurant bills, tipping is not obligatory but it's usual to leave small change (about 5 percent of the bill) on a bar counter, and 5–10 percent on restaurant bills. If you tip taxi drivers, 5 percent is enough. Additional guidelines: hotel porter, per bag, €1; lavatory attendant, 50 cents; tour guide, 10 percent; hairdresser, 10 percent; maid, 60 cents–€1 per day.

TOILETS

Toilet doors are distinguished in Catalan by an 'H' for *Homes* (men) or 'D' for *Dones* (women).

Where are the toilets? **¿Dónde están los servicios?**

TOURIST INFORMATION

Tourist Offices Abroad

Canada: 2 Bloor St West, Suite 3402, Toronto, Ontario M4W 3E2, tel: 416-961 3131.

Ireland: 1, 2 & 3 Westmoreland Street, Dublin, tel: 01-6230 2000.

UK: Spanish Tourist Office, 6th Floor, 64 North Row, London W1K 7DE, tel: 020-7317 2020. This office is open to the public by appointment only.

Catalan Tourist Office: 17 Fleet Street (3rd Floor), London EC4Y 1AA, tel: 020-7583 8855.

US: Water Tower Place, Suite 915 East, 845 North Michigan Avenue, Chicago, IL 60611, tel: 312-642 1992.

8383 Wilshire Boulevard, Suite 960, 90211 Beverly Hills, CA 90211, tel: 323-658 7188.

60 East 42nd Street, 53rd floor, New York, NY 10165, tel: 212-265 8822.

1395 Brickell Avenue, Miami, FL 33131, tel: 305-358 1992.

Barcelona Tourist Offices. The main tourist office is Turisme de Barcelona, Plaça de Catalunya 17, below street level (tel: 93-285 3832; from abroad, tel: 93-285 3834, www.barcelonaturisme.com), open Mon–Sat 8am–8pm, Sun 8am–2pm. The tourism information office in the Ajuntament (Town Hall), Plaça Sant Jaume, is open Mon–Fri 8.30am–8.30pm, Sat 9am–7pm, Sun 9am–2pm. Informació Turística de Catalunya in Palau Robert, Passeig de Gràcia 107 (tel: 93-238 4000; www.gencat.cat), provides information about Catalonia. There are also offices at Sants Station, the airport and on La Rambla.

TRANSPORT

Getting around town is easy, rapid and inexpensive. Transport information: www.tmb.cat or www.renfe.es.

By Metro. The metro (tel: 93-318 7074; www.tmb.cat) is the fastest and easiest way to navigate the city. Stations are marked by a red diamond symbol. The metro runs Mon–Thur, Sun and holidays 5am–midnight, Fri 5am–2am; Sat 24 hours. Maps are available at metro stations, or consult the metro map at the back of this guide.

By Bus (autobús). Barcelona buses (tel: 93-318 7174; www.tmb.cat) have routes and hours clearly marked at the stops. You may have trouble recognising where you are, and most bus drivers speak no English, but buses are a good way of getting to see more of the city. They run daily 5am–11pm (variable depending on route), and there infrequent night buses 10.40pm–5am.

The official Tourist Bus, which passes numerous interesting sights in the city is excellent; you can jump on and off at any stop (see page 122). An air-conditioned bus, rather unfortunately called the 'Tomb Bus', runs during business hours from the Plaça de Catalunya to the uptown Plaça Pius XII, covering all the smart shopping areas.

By Train. FGC (Ferrocarrils Generalitat de Catalunya; tel: 93-205 1515; www.fgc.cat) trains are useful for reaching Barcelona's upper neighbourhoods Sarrià, Pedralbes and Tibidabo, the Parc de Collserola behind Tibidabo and nearby towns such as Sant Cugat, Terrassa and Sabadell. These run from Plaça de Catalunya, but from a different station to the metro. The FGC trains also run from Plaça Espanya to Montserrat, Colònia Güell and other destinations.

Tickets. You can buy a single ticket from the driver on buses, or a multiple card *(tarjeta multi-viaje T10)*, which is punched once you are inside the bus or in an automatic machine as you enter the station. This is valid for bus, metro and urban FGC lines and allows transfer from one means of transport to the other with no extra charge, within a time limit. It works out at nearly half the price of the equivalent in single tickets. Buy the T10 at stations, banks or *estancs*. The T10 can also be used on RENFE trains within Zone 1, which includes the airport.

When's the next bus/train to...? **¿Cuándo sale el próximo autobús/tren para...?**
bus station **estación de autobuses**
A ticket to... **Un billete para...**
single (one-way) **ida**
return (round-trip) **ida y vuelta**
How much is the fare to...? **¿Cuánto es la tarifa a ...?**

By Taxi. Black-and-yellow taxis are everywhere and not too expensive. During the day, they aren't your best option, as traffic is very heavy in the city. At night, especially if you're in the old quarter, taxis are a good option although they have a surcharge. Hail a cab in the street or pick one up where they're lined up. A green light and/or a *libre* (vacant) sign shows when the cab is empty.

Reputable taxi companies include Taxi Amic (tel: 93-420 8088), Radiotaxi 033 (tel: 93-303 3033) and the online company www.bcntaxis.com.

Check the fare before you get in; rates are fixed and are displayed in several languages on the window.

V

VISAS AND ENTRY REQUIREMENTS

Members of EU countries need only a passport. Visas are needed by non-EU nationals unless their country has a reciprocal agreement with Spain.

W

WEBSITES AND INTERNET ACCESS

The following websites provide plenty of useful information:

Barcelona Ajuntament (City Hall): www.bcn.es

Barcelona Tourist Information: www.barcelonaturisme.com

Catalonia on the web: www.gencat.cat

Spain on the web: www.spain.info

National Tourist Office: www.tourspain.es

There are numerous internet cafés and access points in Barcelona, but be aware they are notorious for going out of business.

Y

YOUTH HOSTELS

The following youth hostels get very busy in the summer months, so it is advisable to book in advance: Albergue Juvenil Palau, Carrer Palau 6, tel: 93-412 5080, www.bcnalberg.com; Gothic Point, Carrer Vigatans 5, tel: 93-231 2045, www.equity-point.com; Kabul, Plaça Reial 17, tel: 93-0318 5190, www.kabul.es; Mare de Déu de Montserrat, Mare de Déu de Coll 41–52, tel: 93-210 5151; Pere Tarrès, Numància 149, tel: 93-410 2309, www.peretarres.org/alberg; Point Sea, Plaça del Mar 4, tel: 93-224 7075, www.equity-point.com.

RECOMMENDED HOTELS

Hotels of greatest interest to most visitors are those in the Eixample, the commercial and *modernista* grid north of Plaça de Catalunya, or in the Ciutat Vella (Old Town), which includes La Rambla, Barri Gòtic and the Born. The Old Town provides the best choice of *pensions* and inexpensive hotels, though visitors who stay on or near La Rambla have to tolerate late-night noise and crowds. Likewise, traffic noise can be a problem at many Eixample hotels.

Further away from the centre, better deals are available and these are a good option when you consider that the city's efficient public transport system can whisk you to the centre in a matter of minutes. The most recent additions are along the Waterfront and Diagonal Mar, where high-standard accommodation can be found at a reasonable price. The advantages of sea views and more peaceful nights, not to mention speedy access to the beach, make these areas well worth considering.

The following guide indicates prices for a double room in high season (prices should be used as an approximate guide only):

€€€€	over 200 euros
€€€	140–200 euros
€€	70–140 euros
€	below 70 euros

CIUTAT VELLA

Barceló Raval €€€ *Rambla del Raval 17–21, tel: 93-320 1490*, www.barcelo.com. A cutting-edge high-rise with panoramic views in the middle of El Raval, an indication of moves to smarten up this multicultural district once known as the Barri Xino. Wheelchair access. 186 rooms.

Call € *Carrer de l'Arc de Sant Ramon del Call, tel: 93-302 1123*, www.hotelcall.es. A clean, small, air-conditioned 1-star hotel, located in the shady lanes of the Barri Gòtic. No bar or restaurant but everything you want is on your doorstep. 23 rooms.

Catalonia Portal de l'Àngel €€€ *Portal de l'Àngel 17, tel: 93-318 4141, www. hoteles-catalonia.com.* This charming hotel is housed in a stylish former palace on one of Barcelona's busiest pedestrian shopping streets, close to the Barri Gòtic, La Rambla and the Eixample. The 74 rooms are large and well-furnished, and there's a very pleasant garden patio. It's a good choice if you want to be in the thick of things. Wheelchair access.

Chic&basic Born €€–€€€ *Princesa 50, tel: 93-295 4652, www.chicand basic.com.* This stylish, ultra-modern hotel is in a handsome 19th-century building, well located between the Ciutadella Park and the trendy Born area. Surprisingly good value. 31 rooms.

Chic&basic Zoo €€ *Passeig de Picasso 22, tel: 93-295 4652, www.chicand basic.com.* A pleasant little hotel with 16 rooms and some stylish furnishings, close to the lively nightlife of El Born. It overlooks Ciutadella Park.

Colón €€€ *Avinguda de la Catedral 7, tel: 93-301 1404, www.colonhotel barcelona.com.* This is the closest you can get to the heart of the Barri Gòtic – right across the square from the cathedral. Sixth-floor rooms have large terraces; ask for one with a cathedral view if you make your reservation in time. Given a total renovation, completed in early 2012, the Colón offers stylish furnishings and attention to detail in its 139 rooms.

Cuatro Naciones €€ *La Rambla 40, tel: 93-317 3624, www.h4n.com.* Long-established favourite on the lower half of La Rambla. This means night-time noise, but being right in the heart of things and you get some great views. Wheelchair access. 54 rooms.

Hotel España €€€ *Carrer de Sant Pau 11, tel: 93-550 0000, www.hotel espanya.com.* Just off the lower part of La Rambla, the España may not be the place it once was, but it retains enough flavour of bygone days to recommend it. The beautiful public rooms were designed by *modernista* architect Domènech i Montaner. Completely renovated in 2010, it brings modern chic to a 19th-century building. Wheelchair access. 82 rooms.

Gaudí €€ *Carrer de Nou de la Rambla 12, tel: 93-317 9032*, www.hotel-gaudi.es. Situated opposite one of Gaudí's earliest works, the Palau Güell, and just off La Rambla, with 73 clean, comfortable, simple rooms. Wheelchair access.

Gran Hotel Barcino €€ *Carrer de Jaume I 6, tel: 93-302 2012*, www.hotel-barcino.com. Just off the Plaça de Sant Jaume, right in the heart of the Barri Gòtic, this modern hotel is chic and well designed. The large, airy lobby outclasses the 61 rooms, though.

El Jardí €€ *Plaça Sant Josep Oriol 1, tel: 93-301 5900*, www.eljardi-barcelona.com. Small hotel in the Barri Gòtic, overlooking two of the prettiest plazas in Barcelona. Jardí rooms are a bargain, although a plaza view costs a little more. Popular so book well ahead. 40 rooms.

Neri €€€€ *Carrer de Sant Sever 5, tel: 93-304 0655*, www.hotelneri.com. Elegant boutique hotel in a 17th-century palace overlooking one of the Gothic quarter's most atmospheric squares, near the cathedral. The roof terrace has views over medieval spires. 22 rooms.

Nouvel Hotel €€€ *Carrer de Santa Ana 18–20, tel: 93-301 8274*, www.hotelnouvel.com. On a pedestrianised street between La Rambla and Portal d'Àngel, in an atmospheric area, this small hotel has a wonderful *modernista* lobby and dining room. The 78 rooms are plain, but well equipped.

Ohla €€€€ *Via Laietana 49, tel: 93-341 5050*, www.ohlahotel.com. Opened in 2011, this 5-star hotel occupies a former department store. Behind its neoclassical facade are chic monochrome interiors. Highlights include a Michelin-star restaurant and rooftop deck with glass-sided pool. Wheelchair access. 74 rooms.

Oriente €€€ *Rambla 45–47, tel: 93-302 2558*, www.hotelhusaoriente.com. Nostalgic place located right on La Rambla. Built around a monastic complex, this was Barcelona's first official hotel. Ernest Hemingway and Hans Christian Andersen stayed here (but not together). Lots of character despite recent renovations. 147 rooms.

Peninsular €–€€ *Carrer de Sant Pau 34, tel: 93-302 3138,* www.hotel peninsular.net. In an old Augustinian monastery, with rooms arranged around an inner courtyard. Friendly, helpful staff and good value for money. 59 rooms.

Rembrandt € *Carrer de Portaferrisa 23, tel: 93-318 1011,* www.hostal rembrandt.com. Clean and pleasant if somewhat basic, the family-run Rembrandt is on a pedestrianised street just off La Rambla. Accommodation is up several flights of stairs and not all of the 27 rooms are en suite.

Rivoli Ramblas €€€€ *Rambla 128, tel: 93-481 7676,* www.hotelrivoli ramblas.com. Busy hotel right on La Rambla with good facilities, including a pleasant restaurant, piano bar and a lovely terrace. The style in the 125 rooms ranges from Art Deco to Japanese. Rooms overlooking the courtyard at the back are quieter.

Roma Reial €€ *Plaça Reial 11, tel: 93-302 0366,* www.hotel-romareial. com. The accommodation is basic but the situation, in this buzzing square, makes it a good, cheap option for those who like to be where the action is. 52 rooms.

San Agustí €€ *Plaça Sant Agustí 3, tel: 93-318 1658,* www.hotelsanta gustibarcelona.com. A comfortable, traditional hotel with 77 rooms in a pretty little square near La Rambla. Wheelchair access.

Suizo €€€ *Plaça de l'Àngel 12, tel: 93-310 6108,* www.hotelsuizo.com. Close to the cathedral, and convenient for the Picasso Museum, this intimate, friendly hotel has a turn-of-the-20th-century air. 59 rooms.

EIXAMPLE

Alexandra Hotel €€–€€€ *Carrer de Mallorca 251, tel: 93-467 7166,* www. hotel-alexandra.com. An excellent location for this business-like hotel between Rambla de Catalunya and Passeig de Gràcia. The 109 rooms are not large, but they are comfortable and nicely furnished. Wheelchair access.

Astoria Hotel €€€ *Carrer de París 203, tel: 93-209 8311,* www.derby hotels.com. Part of the prestigious Derby chain, this sophisticated and quiet hotel is just a few paces from prime shopping territory on the Diagonal. Built in the 1950s, the Astoria is elegant and one of the best 3-star hotels in Spain. Some of the 117 rooms have small sitting rooms or garden terraces and there is a roof terrace with small pool.

Avenida Palace Hotel €€€€ *Gran Vía de les Corts Catalanes 605, tel: 93-301 9600,* www.avenidapalace.com. The place to stay if Barcelona's high-tech design craze seems too functional and cold. A luxurious, ornate hotel in the heart of the Eixample, on a busy thoroughfare. The 160 rooms are spacious and elegant. Wheelchair access.

Balmes Hotel €€€ *Carrer de Mallorca 216, tel: 93-451 1914,* www.derby hotels.com. Another Derby Hotel, the Balmes promises 'the advantages of the countryside in the heart of the city', and has an attractive leafy garden and a pool. Close to all the *modernista* masterpieces. It has a collection of African art and contemporary paintings. 102 rooms.

Hotel Casa Fuster €€€€ *Passeig de Gràcia, 132, tel: 93-255 3000,* www. hotelcasafuster.com. A sumptuous, 105-room hotel in a renovated Domènech i Montaner building complete with rooftop pool and views.

Catalonia Plaza Catalunya €€€ *Carrer de Bergara 11, tel: 93-301 5151,* www.hoteles-catalonia.com. A luxury, 4-star hotel just off Plaça de Catalunya, in a handsome 19th-century townhouse expanded to seven floors. The hotel has a relaxed but elegant feel, and service is top-notch, although the 150 rooms are quite small. Swimming pool in an inner courtyard. Wheelchair access.

Claris Hotel €€€€ *Carrer de Pau Claris 150, tel: 93-487 6262,* www. derbyhotels.com. Another in the Derby chain, this is one of Barcelona's most elegant and expensive hotels, in the heart of the Eixample. Very high-tech design behind the facade of the Vedruna Palace and a guests-only museum of Egyptian art. The 124 rooms, many of which are split-level and even two-storey, exude cool chic, combining antiques and Catalan design. Small rooftop pool. Wheelchair access.

Condes de Barcelona Hotel €€€–€€€€ *Passeig de Gràcia 73–5, tel: 93-445 0000*, www.condesdebarcelona.com. With an ultra-chic address, just a block from Gaudí's La Pedrera, this popular hotel occupies two impressive former palaces on opposite corners. The 235 rooms are modern, large and elegant, decorated in bright colours. A favourite of architects and designers, as well as European and Japanese tourists, it boasts a Michelin-star restaurant. Wheelchair access.

Gran Hotel Havana Silken €€€ *Gran Vía de les Corts Catalanes 647, tel: 93-341 7000*, www.hoteles-silken.com. A hip and high-tech hotel in an 1872 mansion with 145 rooms. Barcelona's signature design elements are in every detail. Panoramic roof terrace with pool. Wheelchair access.

Granvia €€€ *Gran Via de les Corts Catalanes 642, tel: 93-318 1900*, www.hotelgranvia.com. A small, intimate hotel with Old World style, occupying a 19th-century palace in a choice location, the Granvia has been operating since the 1930s. Fifty-three smallish but clean rooms, furnished with antiques. Good value. Offers parking and wheelchair access.

Majestic €€€€ *Passeig de Gràcia 68, tel: 93-488 1717*, www.hotelmajestic.es. The Majestic is a large, long-time favourite along one of the city's major shopping streets. Fine dining can be found in the Restaurant Condal, while the Petit Comitè restaurant serves traditional Catalan cuisine. Spa. Wheelchair access. 275 rooms and suites.

Omm €€€€ *Rosselló 265, tel: 93-445 4000*, www.hotelomm.es. Just off Passeig de Gràcia, this award-winning designer hotel is for the chic and beautiful, or those who aspire to be. The 91 rooms are stylish and well lit, the rooftop pool is stunning with views of Gaudí's La Pedrera, and the in-house club is one of the best places to be for Barcelona's night scene. Wheelchair access.

El Palace €€€€ *Gran Via de les Corts Catalanes 668, tel: 93-510 1130*, www.hotelpalacebarcelona.com. A 1919 belle époque hotel, this former Ritz is a classic place to stay. It's ultra-luxurious and white-glove grand, on a splendid tree-lined avenue. Subject to a major renovation, it has competently fused a stylish update with the stunning features of the original building. Some of the 125 rooms have Roman-inspired bathrooms. Michelin-starred restaurant. Wheelchair access.

Regente €€€ *Rambla de Catalunya 76, tel: 93-487 5989*, www.hcchotels. es. A mid-sized hotel in a handsome 1913 *modernista* townhouse on La Rambla de Catalunya. The 79 rooms were refurbished in 2012 and there is a rooftop pool. Wheelchair access.

THE WATERFRONT

Hotel Arts €€€€ *Passeig de la Marina 19–21, tel: 93-221 1000*, www.hotel artsbarcelona.com. The Hotel Arts is a high-tech, deluxe high-rise, situated right on the beach in Vila Olímpica. Extremely efficient, and decorated with sophisticated, understated taste. Large rooms, huge bathrooms and amazing views of the Mediterranean and the city. Wheelchair access. 483 rooms.

Barcelona Princess €€€€ *Avinguda Diagonal 1, tel: 93-356 1000*, www. hotelbarcelonaprincess.com. Situated in the rejuvenated Diagonal Mar district, this cutting-edge hotel has stunning Mediterranean and city views. On the edge of the city but with good metro and tram connections. Good deals available out of season.

W Barcelona €€€€ *Plaça Rosa dels Vents 1, tel: 93-295 2800*, www.w-barcelona.com. Rising high above the Mediterranean like a stylish beacon, the W is in a good beach location great for nightlife, although you may want a taxi to get into town. It's all clean lines and designer chic. Wheelchair access. 473 rooms.

DIAGONAL

Hotel Rey Juan Carlos I €€€€ *Diagonal 661, tel: 93-364 4040*, www.hrjuan carlos.com. Described as Barcelona's only 'urban resort hotel' it is also a premier business choice. Located at the west end of the Diagonal, it offers every amenity a demanding guest could want. Includes 432 rooms, several excellent restaurants, a swimming pool, gardens, fitness centre and spa. Wheelchair access.

INDEX

INSIGHT ⊙ GUIDES POCKET GUIDE

BARCELONA

First Edition 2016
Written by Neil Schlecht
Updated by Magdalena Helsztyńska-Stadnik
Update Production: AM Services
Edited by Kate Drynan
Maps updated by Carte Warsaw
Photography credits: Bigstock 78; Corbis 17, 92; Dreamstime.com 27, 79, 80, 81; Greg Gladman/Apa Publications 2/3M, 4ML, 5MC, 6ML, 7MC, 13, 14, 18, 28/29, 46/47, 66, 72, 74, 75, 82, 84, 88, 98, 100/101, 102; Gregory Wrona/Apa Publications 1, 2MC, 2ML, 2/3T, 3TC, 2/3M, 2/3M, 2/3M, 4/5M, 4/5T, 5TC, 33, 34, 38, 40, 41, 42/43, 45, 48, 50, 52, 53, 58, 60, 61, 62/63, 64, 67, 68, 70, 71, 87, 90; iStockphoto 2TL, 2TC, 4ML, 4MR, 4TL, 4TL, 6TL, 7MC, 7TC, 10, 21, 22, 24, 26, 30, 30/31, 36/37, 55, 56/57, 76, 94/95, 96/97; Mark Read/Apa Publications 32
Cover picture: iStock
All Rights Reserved
© 2016 Apa Digital (CH) AG and Apa Publications (UK) Ltd

Distribution
UK, Ireland and Europe: Apa Publications (UK) Ltd; sales@insightguides.com
United States and Canada: Ingram Publisher Services; ips@ingramcontent.com
Australia and New Zealand: Woodslane; info@woodslane.com.au

Southeast Asia: Apa Publications (SN) Pte; singaporeoffice@insightguides.com
Hong Kong, Taiwan and China: Apa Publications (HK) Ltd; hongkongoffice@insightguides.com
Worldwide: Apa Publications (UK) Ltd; sales@insightguides.com

Special Sales, Content Licensing and CoPublishing
Insight Guides can be purchased in bulk quantities at discounted prices. We can create special editions, personalised jackets and corporate imprints tailored to your needs. sales@insightguides.com; www.insightguides.biz

Printed in Poland

No part of this book may be reproduced, stored in a retrieval system or transmitted in any form or means electronic, mechanical, photocopying, recording or otherwise, without prior written permission from Apa Publications.

Contact us
Every effort has been made to provide accurate information in this publication, but changes are inevitable. The publisher cannot be responsible for any resulting loss, inconvenience or injury. We would appreciate it if readers would call our attention to any errors or outdated information. We also welcome your suggestions; please contact us at: hello@insightguides.com www.insightguides.com

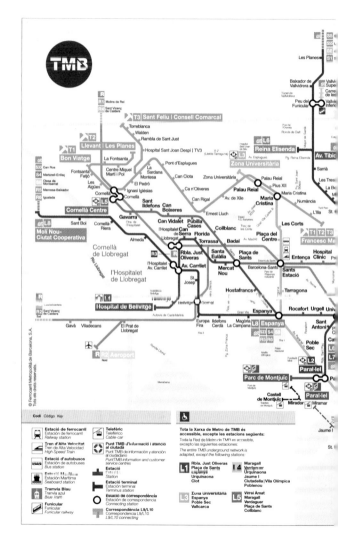

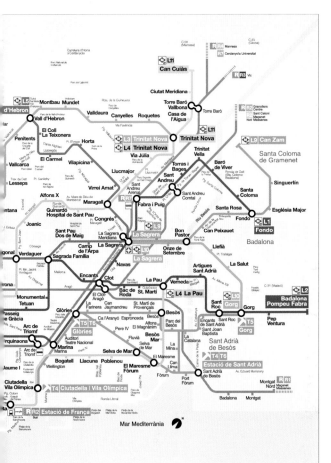

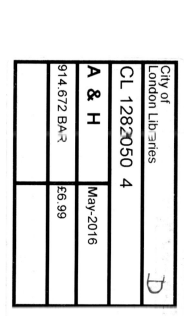